BASIC GOALS IN
SPELLING

SEVENTH EDITION

WILLIAM KOTTMEYER AND AUDREY CLAUS

Webster Division, McGraw-Hill Book Company

Ne York   St. Louis   San Francisco   Dallas   Atlanta

William Kottmeyer, former Superintendent of the St. Louis Public Schools, is a nationally recognized educational innovator. His spelling and reading publications have received high acclaim for nearly four decades. Dr. Kottmeyer is currently an author-in-residence in the Webster Division.

Audrey Claus is a former teacher and administrator in the St. Louis Public Schools. Miss Claus is co-author of five editions of this spelling series and several reading programs. She, too, is currently an author-in-residence in the Webster Division.

Project Director: Virginia S. Brown
Sponsoring Editor: Martha Alderson
Editing Supervisor: Bea Rockstroh
Designers: E. Rohne Rudder and Donna Stephens
Production Manager: Tom Goodwin

The photos in this book are by Gary Brady, 29, 30, 95, 99, 105, 124; Walter Chandoha, 77, 81, 91; *Bruce Coleman/* Jen and Des Bartlett, 47; K.W. Fink, 56; Michael Gadomski, 71; Laura Riley, 67; Norman Owen Tohalin, 114; E.R. Degginger, 8, 57; Phil Degginger, 38; Al Gardner, 28; Brian Gordon, 119, 123; Dwight Kuhn, 57; Robert Lee III, 137, 141; Frank Oberle, Jr., 3, 5, 7, 12, 15, 16, 18, 20, 33, 37, 38, 40, 42, 43, 46, 51, 65, 66, 72, 74, 76, 82, 85, 86, 90, 94, 100, 104, 129, 133, 146, 149, 150, 153, 154, 157, 161, 165; *Photo Researchers/*T. Angermayer, 32; Bill Curtsinger, cover, i, ii, 2, 3, 21; S. McCartney, 77; Robert Noonan, 110; Carleton Ray, 24; Wm. Townsend, Jr., 52; Lewis Portnoy, 62, 115, 142, 145, 158, 162; St. Louis Zoological Park, 25; David Tylka, 61, 128. Photo research by E. Rohne Rudder.

The illustrations were created by Barbara Pritzen and Blanche Sims.
The cover design is by E. Rohne Rudder.

The authors are indebted to Scott, Foresman and Company for permission to use and to adapt definitions from the *Thorndike-Barnhart Intermediate Dictionary* and *Thorndike-Barnhart Advanced Dictionary* by E. L. Thorndike and Clarence L. Barnhart. Copyright © 1979 by Scott, Foresman and Company.

TABLE OF CONTENTS

HANDWRITING MODELS

a b c d e f g h i

j k l m n o p q r

s t u v w x y z

A B C D E F G H I

J K L M N O P Q R

S T U V W X Y Z

2

1 Fast Skates

The vowel sound in **fast** is called **short a**.
We show **short a** like this: /a/.
We spell /a/ with the letter **a**.

The vowel sound in **skate** is called **long a**.
We show **long a** like this: /ā/.
We spell /ā/ like this:

| **ai** | **ay** | a-consonant-e |

flat
past
land
drag
rail
claim
gain
fail
laid
clay
tray
lay
spray
plate
lake
snake
hate
brave
ᔕ great
ᔕ have

1. Say the words. Listen for the vowel sounds.

2. First write the word that means "pull."
Then write the four other /a/ words.

flat
past
land
drag
rail
claim
gain
fail
laid
clay
tray
lay
spray
plate
lake
snake
hate
brave
great
have

3. First write the word that means "sprinkle."
Then write the other **ay** words.

4. First write the word that means "bold."
Then write the other **a**-consonant-**e** words.

5. First write the word that means "placed," or
"put down." Then write the other **ai** words.

Ⓢ *A **snurk** is a word with an unexpected spelling.
Why do we call **great** and **have** snurks?*

6. Write **great, have,** and **gain.** Circle the /ā/ words.

7. Write the picture words. Circle the plural words.

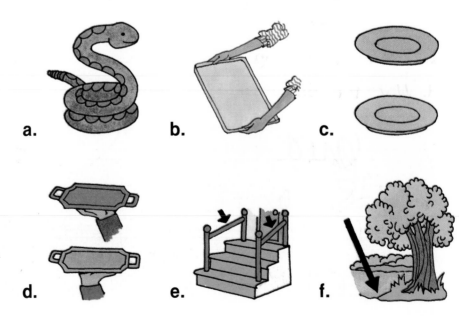

a.

b.

c.

d.

e.

f.

Words in a dictionary are called **entry words.** Symbols between slant marks show the <u>sounds</u> in each word.

Dictionary Skills

plate /plāt/

These dictionary signs stand for consonant sounds:

/b/ **brave** /d/ **day** /f/ **fail**
/g/ **gain** /h/ **hay** /j/ **jay**
/l/ **lake** /m/ **mail** /n/ **nail**
/p/ **paid** /r/ **rake** /s/ **sail**
/t/ **take** /v/ **vase** /w/ **way**

1. Write the words that start with these sounds.

/k/   /f/   /s/

2. Write the rhyming **ai** words.

3. Write the four **ay** words in alphabetical order.

*The dictionary sign for a long-vowel sound has a small line, or **macron,** over the vowel letter.* /ā/ *In most dictionaries, the sign for a short-vowel sound has no mark over the vowel letter.* /a/

Spelling Helps Language

An **abbreviation** is a shortened form of a word. **Mr.** is the abbreviation for **Mister.** The abbreviation **Mr.** begins with a capital letter and usually ends with a period. **Mr.** is only used with a person's name, as when we write **Mr. Ray Wade** or **Mr. J. T. Crane.**

1. Write a sentence about men named Blake and Gray who sailed all day on a lake. Use **Mr.** and five /ā/ words.

2. **Proofreading** means "reading to find mistakes." Proofread these sentences to find two punctuation mistakes and three misspelled words. Write the sentences correctly.

> 1. Jan clames to have some
>   fine land on that lake
> 2. Mr. Grant has a great stack
>   of plats on a tray.
> 3. Some plant can grow in clay

Word Wu??le

gra snake ss

a ___ in

the ___

6

Spelling Helps Reading

Sound out the words.

blast	slant	slam	waist	base	fade	trail
pray	sway	way	stain	pay	grape	date
bait	braid	brain	gray	cast	cab	strap
crate	cane	blame	crab	faint	hay	trap

Complete the sentences correctly.

1. **Tray** is to **plate** as **sack** is to...

    a. grain   **b.** (bag)   **c.** lake

2. **Hand** is to **wave** as **tail** is to...

    a. snake   **b.** tame   **c.** wag

3. **Spade** is to **sand** as **rake** is to...

    a. hay   **b.** nail   **c.** vase

4. **Glad** is to **sad** as **pass** is to...

    a. fail   **b.** gain   **c.** play

5. **Mask** is to **face** as **band** is to...

    a. grass   **b.** flake   **c.** hat

6. **Match** is to **flame** as **sprain** is to...

    a. race   **b.** pain   **c.** shame

7. **Brake** is to **train** as **latch** is to...

    a. chain   **b.** stay   **c.** gate

Test

7

nest
bend
slept
mend
spell
green
seed
sweet
speech
deep
teeth
teach
neat
cream
reach
meal
wheat
east
 dead
 bread

2 Web Feet

*The vowel sound in **web** is called **short e**.*
We show it like this: /e/.
We spell /e/ with the letter e.

*The vowel sound in **feet** is called **long e**.*
We show it like this: /ē/.
We can spell /ē/ like this:

ee   **ea**

1. Say the words. Listen for the vowel sounds.

2. First write the word that means "fix."
Then write the six other /e/ words.

8

3. Write the snurks. Underline the letters that spell /e/.

4. First write the word that names a grain. Then write the six other **ea** words.

5. First write the word that means "a talk." Then write the five other **ee** words.

6. Write the words that start with /t/ in alphabetical order. Use the third letter in each word.

 Working with the Words

Dictionary Skills

Each dictionary sign stands for one sound, no matter how the sound is spelled. **ll** spells the sound that ends **spell**. **l** spells the sound that ends **meal**.

spell /spel/   **meal** /mēl/

1. Write the correct spelling for /spel/ and /mēl/.

2. Write **slept, reach,** and **wheat.** Circle /hwēt/.

nest
bend
slept
mend
spell
green
seed
sweet
speech
deep
teeth
teach
neat
cream
reach
meal
wheat
east
dead
bread

3. Write the sentences. Underline the /ē/ words.

    a. This wheat bread tastes great.

    b. He keeps his desk neat and clean.

 *Spelling Helps Language*

> **Mrs.** and **Miss** are abbreviations of **Mistress.**
> **Mrs.** is used with the name of a married woman
> and **Miss** with the name of an unmarried woman.
> **Mrs.** usually has a period, but **Miss** does not.
> **Mrs.** and **Miss** both start with capital **M.**

1. Write a sentence telling that Mr. Breen, his wife, and daughter Jean had a meal of beef, peas, fresh green beans, and peaches with cream. Use three abbreviations.

2. Proofread this shopping list. Write it right.

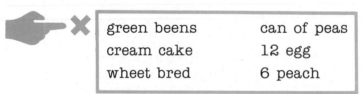

green beens	can of peas
cream cake	12 egg
wheet bred	6 peach

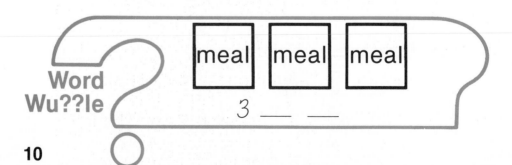

Word Wu??le

meal meal meal

3 ___ ___

Spelling Helps Reading

Sound out the words.

web	screen	lend	scream	seem	swell	beast
creep	sweep	when	steep	greet	least	week
meat	feast	leaf	shell	stream	treat	depth
swept	egg	peel	peek	streak	read	dream

Choose the word in each row that does not belong.

1. geese (bees) cranes quail hens
2. ants sheep cats rats snakes
3. bed desk lamp chest tent
4. feet hands legs meals necks
5. beans streams peaches peas beets
6. meat beef cheese ham veal
7. squeak smell squeal scream yell
8. sleet trees plants weeds grass
9. sand lake sea stream creek
10. squeeze grasp grab heal clasp

Dictionaries show the **wh** sound as /hw/. We say /h/ and then /w/ in words like **when** and **wheat**. Some people skip /h/ and say /wen/ and /wēt/. How do you say **when** and **wheat?**

Test

slim
sting
skill
pinch
stripe
whine
wise
strike
pride
tight
sight
slight
fright
sigh
thigh
tried
dried
lied
 build
 child

3 Swift Ride Words

The vowel sound in **swift** is called **short i.**

We show it like this: /**i**/.

We spell /**i**/ with the letter **i.**

The vowel sound in **ride** is called **long i.**

We show it like this: /**ī**/.

We can spell /**ī**/ like this:

| **i**-consonant-**e** | **igh** | **ie** |

1. Say the words. Listen for the vowel sounds.

2. Write the word that means "thin" and the other /i/ words. One word is a snurk.

12

3. First write the word that means "a scare."
Then write the five other **igh** words.

4. First write the word that means "hit."
Then write the other **i**-consonant-**e** words.

5. Write the word that means "said something
not true." Then write the other **ie** words.

Working with the Words

**Dictionary
Skills**

These dictionary signs stand for the
sounds that start the picture words.

 /sh/

shine /shīn/

 /ch/

pinch /pinch/

 /th/

thigh /thī/

1. Write the words with /ch/, /th/, and /hw/.

2. Unscramble the letters to spell one snurk and
two /ē/ words from Unit 2.

    a. theet   **b.** weath   **c.** dilch

3. Write **tied** and the words that rhyme with **tied.**

13

slim
sting
skill
pinch
stripe
whine
wise
strike
pride
tight
sight
slight
fright
sigh
thigh
tried
dried
lied
build
child

Spelling Helps Language

Ms. is a short form for **Miss** and **Mrs.** The abbreviation **Ms.** may be used before any woman's name. It is pronounced /miz/. **Ms.** may be written with a period or without a period.

1. Write a sentence about Fran Brill who has great skill in building fine kites. Use **Ms.**

2. **Proofread** Mike's note. He used periods and commas correctly in this note, but he made other mistakes. Write the note correctly.

Dear sis,
   Thanks for the fine red and white tie. I like ties with wide strips. It looked just right when I tryed it on last night.
                              Mike

Word Wu??le

skate
―――――
thin ice

___ on ___ ___

14

Spelling Helps Reading

Sound out the words.

split	cling	shift	twist	sling	spite	spies
drip	tribe	file	high	lies	right	skid
pile	quite	might	wife	fight	mile	bright
fine	fried	cries	hiss	rise	flies	fist

Write **T** or **F** for each sentence.

1. We like flying kites in the springtime.
2. Five times three is less than nine and five.
3. A ten-mile hike will tire a sick child.
4. "Strike three!" will make the man at bat smile.
5. We try to find steel in tin mines.
6. Five slices of pie might make a child ill.
7. A man might like a bright tie with wide stripes.
8. We need ripe grapes on the vines to make fine jam.
9. A fine man will take pride in a life of crime.
10. The flag has six white and nine red stripes.
11. Five and nine is less than nine times three.
12. A kite can fly as high as a plane.

Two more ways to spell an /ī/?
In **dry** and **cry** you can see a **y.**
And just an **i** in words like **find**
And **grind** and **mind** and **kind** and **blind.**

Test

odd
flock
prompt
lost
frost
loss
note
chose
stroke
stole
toast
coal
coast
coach
crow
bowl
fold
bold

4 Cold Snow Cones

The vowel sound in **hot** is called **short o: /o/.**
In some words **short o** has the sound we hear
in **dog.** We show it like this: **/ô/.**
We spell **/o/** and **/ô/** with the letter **o.**

The vowel sound in **cone** is called **long o.**
We show it like this: **/ō/.**
We spell **/ō/** like this:

o-consonant-**e** **cone**	**o** before **ld** **cold**
oa **toast**	**ow** **snow**

gone
most

1. Say the words. Listen for the vowel sounds.

16

2. Write the /o/ and /ô/ words, including a snurk.

3. First write the word that means "picked out." Then write the other **o**-consonant-**e** words.

4. First write the word that means "train a team." Then write the three other **oa** words.

5. Write **crow, bowl, most, fold,** and **bold** in alphabetical order. Underline the two words that rhyme.

6. Write **lost, frost,** and **most** in alphabetical order. Underline the two words that rhyme.

Working with the Words

Dictionary Skills

Entry words in a dictionary are in alphabetical order. Words that start with the same letter are arranged according to the second letter. When the first two or three letters are the same, the words are arranged by the third or fourth letter.

coach   coal   coast

odd
flock
prompt
lost
frost
loss
note
chose
stroke
stole
toast
coal
coast
coach
crow
bowl
fold
bold
gone
most

1. Write **frost, flock,** and **fold** in alphabetical order. Underline the /ō/ word.

2. Write **chose, crow, coach, coal,** and **coast** in the order they come in the Spelling Dictionary. Underline the /k/ words.

3. Write the questions. Underline the /ō/ words.

   a. Do most crows go in flocks?

   b. Do we have frost when it is cold?

4. Write the words with these meanings.

   a. on time   **b.** brave   **c.** strange

   d. group of sheep   **e.** short letter   **f.** crease

5. Write the words with the <u>opposite</u> meanings.

   a. found   **b.** least   **c.** gain

*The dictionary sign for the vowel sound in **lost** has a "tent" over the letter **o.***

*The "tent" is called a **circumflex.** /ô/*

18

Spelling Helps Language

Dr. is the abbreviation for **Doctor.** The abbreviation **Dr.** is used only with a person's name, as when we write **Dr. Rose Stone** or **Dr. Moss.** We never use **Dr.** in a sentence without the doctor's name.

1. Write a sentence about a doctor named Joan Sill who told Bob Stone to eat toast. Use **Dr.** and **Mr.**

2. Write a sentence about Joan Oaks who wants to be a doctor when she grows up. Do <u>not</u> use any abbreviations.

3. **Proofread** this news story and write it correctly.

> Tom Fox Breaks Leg
> Coach Chuck Jones said today that Tom Fox could not play on the class baseball teem for some time. Tom brok his leg when he stole home in a bold play in the game last week. The Dr. notes that the bone needs at least ten weaks to mend.

Word Wu??le

3 ₁ 7 ends
5 9 ends
___ *and* ___

Spelling Helps Reading

Sound out the words.

those	throat	thrown	stove	boss	roast	hold
globe	slope	trot	lock	rose	goal	gold
joke	row	oak	hog	woke	grown	blow
cone	moss	fond	boast	chop	groan	gong

Choose the word in List B that fits with the words in List A.

A | | | **B** | |
|---|---|---|---|---|---|
| **1.** sleet | frost | snow | (cold) | road | pond |
| **2.** roach | moth | ant | dog | frog | flea |
| **3.** coat | robe | cloak | rose | cape | pot |
| **4.** scrub | mop | pail | roast | toad | soap |
| **5.** throat | nose | neck | leg | teeth | thigh |
| **6.** blocks | doll | top | kite | fox | lock |
| **7.** toast | bread | cake | oats | crop | pie |
| **8.** flock | mob | team | gang | show | boat |
| **9.** goat | dog | frog | bone | hog | rope |
| **10.** globe | dome | bowl | cross | pot | lot |
| **11.** groan | moan | croak | scream | hold | throw |
| **12.** glow | flame | blaze | smoke | rose | home |

Test

5 Cute New Pup Words

bulb
grunt
clutch
dump
huge
rude
cute
cube
few
drew
stew
chew
crew
glue
clue
true
suit
bruise
§ *truth*
§ *does*

The vowel sound in **cub** is called **short u**.
We show **short u** like this: /u/.
We spell /u/ with the letter **u**.

The vowel sound in **cute** is called **long u**.
We show **long u** like this: /ū/.
In some words **long u** has the sound we hear in **true**. We show the vowel sound in **true** like this: /ü/.
We spell /ū/ or /ü/ like this:

| u-consonant-e | ew | ui | ue |

1. Write the word that means "hold." Then write the four other short-**u** words. Circle the snurk.

bulb
grunt
clutch
dump
huge
rude
cute
cube
few
drew
stew
chew
crew
glue
clue
true
suit
bruise
truth
does

2. First write the word that means "not many."
Then write the four other **ew** words.

3. First write the word that means "very big."
Then write the three other **u**-consonant-**e** words.

4. Write the **ui** words, the **ue** words, and the /ü/
snurk. Circle the word that means "hurt."

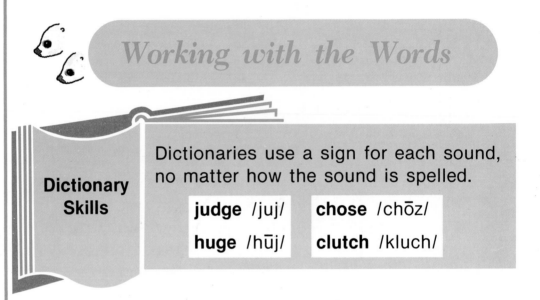

Working with the Words

Dictionary Skills

Dictionaries use a sign for each sound,
no matter how the sound is spelled.

| **judge** /juj/ | **chose** /chōz/ |
| **huge** /hūj/ | **clutch** /kluch/ |

1. Write the five /k/ words in alphabetical order.

2. Two words start with /s/. Two words end with /z/.
Write these four words in alphabetical order.

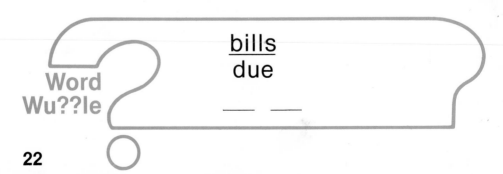

Word
Wu??le

bills
due

___ ___

22

3. Write the sentences. Use punctuation marks and capital letters correctly. Circle the /ū/ or /ü/ words.

   a. does a cube have six flat sides

   b. my new blue suit has a few spots

4. Write a sentence telling how many sides a cube has. (Use the Spelling Dictionary.)

 Spelling Helps Language

A.M. is the abbreviation for Latin words that mean "before noon." We may write **A.M.** or **a.m.** to show time from midnight to noon.
P.M. is the abbreviation for Latin words that mean "after noon." We may write **P.M.** or **p.m.** to show time from noon to midnight.

1. Write these words and abbreviations in alphabetical order: **A.M., P.M., Dr., dump, plum,** and **prune.**

2. Proofread Sue's treasure-hunt note. Find five mistakes. Write the note correctly.

Meet at Ms. Lunt's fruit stand at 9 am. Go a few blocks west to a huge blew plum tree. You will find three grate new clue stuck to the tree trunk their.

Sound out these words. Then read the verse aloud.

stump	tube	fruit	threw	fuse	flew	mule
skunk	shrewd	rule	grew	crutch	trust	trunk
crude	punch	flute	news	blue	tune	dull

Oh, the long-vowel words! I wish they'd say
That we may spell them just one way.
But **bake** and **chain** and **bait** and **plate?**
And **take** and **pain** and **gate** and **wait?**
Our beets are red, our trees are green.
But beans are cheap and streams are clean!
I wind the twine and fly my kite.
I bide my time. Night lights are bright.
The snow is cold. Throw me my coat.
Old moles dig holes. Our boat will float.
Will mules chew fruit? Are flute tunes true?
Do dudes wear suits? Is prune juice blue?
Oh, the long-vowel words! I wish they'd say
That we may spell them just one way!

The dictionary sign for the vowel sound

in **rude** is a "two-dot **u**." /ü/

Test

24

6 Small Hoot Owl Noise

/ü/ shows the vowel sound in **hoot**.

/u̇/ shows the vowel sound in **crook**.

We spell /ü/ and /u̇/ with   oo .

/ou/ shows the vowel sound in **owl**.

We spell /**ou**/ with   ou   or   ow .

/oi/ shows the vowel sound in **noise**.

We spell /**oi**/ with   oy   or   oi .

/ô/ shows the vowel sound in **small**.

We spell /ô/ with   a before l   ,   aw   ,

or   au .

spoon
tool
smooth
hoof
crook
noun
south
plow
howl
gown
soil
coil
claw
thaw
haunt
pause
stall
halt
▽ through
▽ thought

1. Write the seven /ô/ words including one snurk.

spoon
tool
smooth
hoof
crook
noun
south
plow
howl
gown
soil
coil
claw
thaw
haunt
pause
stall
halt
through
thought

2. Write the /ou/ words. Circle the word for "dress."

3. Write the /ù/ and /ü/ words including the snurk. Circle the word that means "a bent part."

4. Write the /oi/ words. Circle the word for "dirt."

 *Say **thought** and **through.** What sound do we expect **ou** to spell? Why are **thought** and **through** snurks?*

5. Write **thought, through,** and **threw.** Underline the words with the same pronunciation.

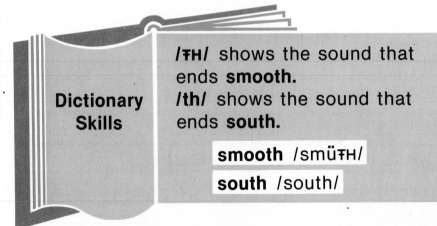

Working with the Words

Dictionary Skills

/ŦH/ shows the sound that ends **smooth.**
/th/ shows the sound that ends **south.**

smooth /smüŦH/

south /south/

1. Write the spelling words that have the **th** letters. Underline the word that has the /ŦH/ sound.

2. A **noun** is a "naming" word. Write these nouns.

a.    b.   c.

Spelling Helps Language

The dictionary uses the abbreviation **n.** for **noun.**

hoof /hu̇f/ *n.* Hard cover on some animals' feet.

1. Find **booth, brow,** and **hawk** in the dictionary.
Write the words that are shown as nouns.

2. **Proofread** this test and write the test correctly.
Mark each sentence **True** or **False.**

> 1. A noun is a naming word.
> 2. A hoof is the same as a klaw.
> 3. the words *thaw* and *freeze* have
>   the same meaning.

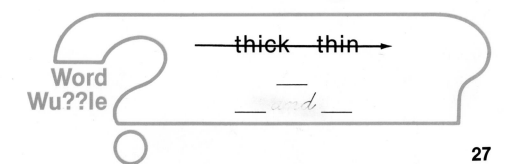

**Word
Wu??le**

~~thick   thin~~ →

___

__ *and* __

27

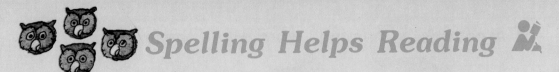
Sound out the words. Then read the verse.

hood	bloom	false	cloud	small	shook	droop
stout	soot	booth	scoop	pound	couch	hawk
bound	caught	drawn	mount	salt	brow	growl

The proper way to spell an /ü/?
Just use the **o**'s—not one, but two.
So pools are cool and the red rose blooms.
So a goose may roost, and the brides have grooms.
Of course, the **o**'s spell /u̇/ in **brook,**
So we often look at a good cookbook.
One proper way to spell the /ou/
You see in **"Wow! How now, brown cow?"**
But with **o-u** in **found** and **house,**
In **bound** and **sound** and **round** and **mouse.**
For /oi/, my friend, you have a choice:
See **boy** and **toy** and **oil** and **voice.**
Then there's the /ô/ you hear in **all.**
But have a look at **haul** and **crawl.**
Have ears like hawks and eyes like owls
And watch out for two-letter vowels.

The sound sign in look is "one-dot u." /u̇/

Test

7 More Large Rare Birds

> All words in the spelling list have vowel-r sounds.
>
> **/är/** shows the vowel-r sounds in **large**.
>
> We spell **/är/** with **ar** .
>
> **/ãr/** shows the vowel-r sounds in **rare**.
>
> We spell **/ãr/** with **are** and **air** .
>
> **/ôr/** shows the vowel-r sounds in **more**.
>
> We spell **/ôr/** with **or** , **ore** , or **oar** .
>
> **/èr/** shows the vowel-r sound in **bird**.
>
> We spell **/èr/** with **ir** , **ur** , or **er** .

card
dart
quart
porch
horn
core
chore
roar
oar
spare
glare
chair
air
curve
urge
firm
verb
germ
 *world*
 worse

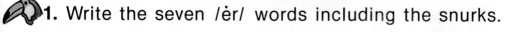 **1.** Write the seven /èr/ words including the snurks.

2. Write the three /är/ words. Underline the <u>verb</u>.

3. Write the six /ôr/ words. Underline the <u>verbs</u>.

4. Write the four /ãr/ words. Underline /glãr/.

*Which sounds do you expect **or** to spell?*
*Why are **world** and **worse** called snurks?*

 Working with the Words

Dictionary Skills

Dictionaries give one or more meanings for each entry word.

card /kärd/ *n.* **1.** A flat piece of stiff paper. **2.** One of a pack of cards used in games.

1. Write **horn, world,** and **quart.** Write the number of meanings the Spelling Dictionary gives.

2. Write the four vowel-**r** picture words.

a. b. c. d.

Spelling Helps Language

The dictionary uses the abbreviation **v.** for **verb.** The **v.** after the entry word tells that the entry word is used as a verb.

pare /pãr/ *v.* Peel; cut off the outer part.

1. Find **dart, soar, horn, north,** and **whirl** in the Spelling Dictionary. Write the words that are shown as verbs.

2. **Proofread** this alphabetical list of words. Find mistakes in spelling and alphabetizing. Write the list correctly.

1. core	5. prompt	9. dart
2. card	6. roar	10. urge
3. glew	7. quart	11. world
4. gain	8. spare	12. verb

card
dart
quart
porch
horn
core
chore
roar
oar
spare
glare
chair
air
curve
urge
firm
verb
germ
world
worse

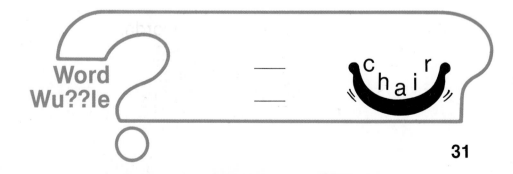

Word Wu??le ___ ___

Sound out these words. Read the poem aloud.

cord	square	thirst	whirl	scarf	spur	burn
torch	tore	squirm	thorn	barge	fort	shark
purse	sport	rare	clerk	nerve	score	third

Girls: Oh, sneaky **R,** you're out of bounds!
Why change our lovely vowel sounds?
You pounce on /a/ and make it /är/
To make us say **jar, car,** and **star.**
You steal three more and make them /ėr/
In **her, girl, curl.** How dare you, Sir?

Boys: You grab our /o/ and make it /ôr/
In **more** and **oar** and words like **for.**
You take our /ā/ and leave us /âr/
In **chair** and **care.** That isn't fair!

All: For what you do to vowel sounds,
It seems to us that we have grounds
To shut you up, to make you sweat,
To drop you from our alphabet!

The dictionary sign for the vowel sound in **fair** has a wavy line, or **tilde,** over the letter **a. /âr/**

Test

32

8 Swimming and Diving

We double the final consonant before **ing** in short-vowel words that end with one consonant.

swim **swimming**

We drop the **e** before **ing** in long-vowel words that end with silent **e**.

dive **diving**

flapping
budding
propping
wedding
sledding
skidding
fanning
gripping
humming
shapping
risping
dozping
chokping
tunping
breathping
bathping
dinping
squeezping
⑤ putting
⑤ provping

1. Write the **ing** words with doubled-consonant letters. Circle the snurk.

2. Write the /a/ and /i/ words without **ing** endings.

3. Write the /ā/, /ē/, and /ī/ words with **ing** endings.

4. Write **choke, tune, prove,** and **doze** with **ing** endings.

 Working with the Words

Dictionary Skills

Dictionaries show the **ing** and **ed** forms of words that double the final consonant before **ing** and **ed**.

skid /skid/ *v.* Slide to the side. **skidded, skidding.**

Dictionaries show the **ing** and **ed** forms of words that drop the final silent **e** before **ing** and **ed**.

bathe /bāŦH/ *v.* Take or give a bath. **bathed, bathing.**

1. Find **grip, breathe,** and **dart** in the Spelling Dictionary. Write the words for which the **ed** form is shown. Then write the **ed** forms.

2. Find **howl, mean, prove,** and **put** in the dictionary. Write the words for which the **ing** form is shown. Then write the **ing** forms.

3. Write the words for these meanings. Some will have **ed** or **ing** endings.

    a. eating dinner   **b.** ate dinner

    c. marry   **d.** riding a sled

    e. blew air in and out   **f.** sleeping lightly

    g. swinging about loosely   **h.** took a bath

    i. slept lightly   **j.** putting out buds

flap
bud
prop
wed
sled
skid
fan
grip
hum
shape
rise
doze
choke
tune
breathe
bathe
dine
squeeze
put
prove

Spelling Helps Language

The abbreviations **sing.** and **pl.** are used in many dictionaries.

    sing. stands for **singular,** "only one."

    pl. stands for **plural,** "more than one."

1. Write **wedding, buds, sleds, geese, goose,** and **tune.** Beside each word write **sing.** or **pl.** to show whether it is a singular or plural noun.

35

2. Unscramble the words in the speech balloon to write the sentence telling what Fran said. The period at the end of the sentence goes inside the quotation marks.

should be not You dozing job on the

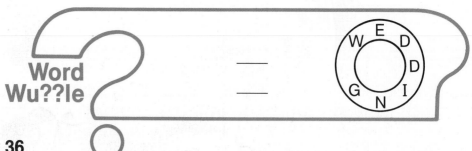

Fran said to Ben, "_____."

3. Remember, a **synonym** is a word that means the same, or nearly the same, as another word. **Proofread** this list of synonyms to find four mistakes. Write the list correctly.

1. spinning — peeling
2. dineing — eating
3. geting — gaining
4. melting — thawing
5. saying — suiting
6. paring — whirling
7. fitting — stating

Word Wu??le

W E D
D
G N I

Spelling Helps Reading

Sound out the words.

slapping	betting	spinning	nodding	scrubbing
curving	halting	sliding	making	using
planning	testing	driving	trapping	shining
slipping	freezing	getting	whining	coding

Complete the sentences correctly.

1. **Wing** is to **flapping** as **hand** is to...
       a. rising   **b.** slapping   **c.** biting

2. **Top** is to **spinning** as **blade** is to...
       a. shaving   **b.** making   **c.** ruling

3. **Sled** is to **sliding** as **car** is to...
       a. running   **b.** stopping   **c.** skipping

4. **Feet** are to **hiking** as **arms** are to...
       a. swimming   **b.** smiling   **c.** choosing

5. **Lungs** are to **breathing** as **eyes** are to...
       a. dozing   **b.** gazing   **c.** stroking

6. **Cakes** are to **baking** as **cubes** are to...
       a. freezing   **b.** liking   **c.** fanning

7. **Brushes** are to **scrubbing** as **spades** are to...
       a. batting   **b.** digging   **c.** filing

Test

37

sunshine
necktie
mankind
crossroads
classmate
midnight
teapot
railroad
bluejay
bedtime
blindfold
homesick
newsreel
skyline
suitcase
grown-up
well-made
useless

Compound words are made by putting shorter words together.
Each short word forms an **eye-syllable,** or word part, that you can see.

sail̖boat

We spell the long-vowel and short-vowel eye-syllables in compounds as we spell one-syllable words.

1. Write the ten compound words in which the <u>first</u> word part has a short-vowel sound.

2. Write the ten compound words in which the <u>first</u> word part has a long-vowel sound.

3. Write the words with the /ā/ sound in one word part.

Working with the Words

Dictionary Skills

When a word has more than one syllable, we usually say one syllable louder than the other. A heavy **accent mark** shows the loud syllable. We call the heavy accent mark a **primary accent.**

useless /ūs′ ləs/   **instead** /in sted′/

Compound words often have two accent marks. The primary accent shows the louder syllable. A lighter accent mark, called a **secondary accent,** shows a softer syllable.

necktie /nek′ tī′/   **crossroads** /krôs′ rōdz′/

1. Write , , and .
Circle each word part with a secondary accent.

2. Write the compound words with these meanings.
Circle each word part with a primary accent.

 a. longing for home   **b.** 12 o'clock at night

 c. not useful   **d.** no longer a child

 e. made with care   **f.** all people

 g. time for bed   **h.** cover the eyes

*Some compounds have a small line, called
a* **hyphen,** *between the word parts.*

made-up /mād′ up′/ *adj.* Not real.

3. Write the spelling words that have hyphens.

Spelling Helps Language

1. Write two or three sentences about a grown-up
whose train ticket is locked in a suitcase. Use at
least five of these words and any others you need:
Ms., railroad, suitcase, helpless, careless,
and **cannot.**

The abbreviation **adj.** stands for **adjective,** a "describing word."

homesick /hōm′ sik′/ *adj.* Sad because home is far away.

2. Write **useless, made-up, skyline, old-time,** and **homemade.** Underline the words that the Spelling Dictionary shows as adjectives.

3. **Proofread** the two lists of compounds. List A has spelling mistakes. List B has mixed-up word parts. Write both lists correctly.

a	*B*
1. *rainbow*	1. *goldshield*
2. *hanbag*	2. *windsick*
3. *newscast*	3. *homefish*
4. *oatmeal*	4. *mailstead*
5. *blewjay*	5. *inbox*

sun shine
neck tie
man kind
cross roads
class mate
mid night
tea pot
rail road
blue jay
bed time
blind fold
home sick
news reel
sky line
suit case
grown-up
well-made
use less
wind shield
in stead

Word Wu??le

r
o
roads
d
s

___

41

 # Spelling Helps Reading

Sound out these words. Then read the story.

became	fusebox	plaything	wishbone	homemade
goldfish	lowland	fruitcake	newscast	grindstone
myself	spotlight	blueprint	mailbox	made-up
show-off	bedtime	sailboat	longhand	rowboat

Jack Carson and his classmate, Edwin Wainright, had planned a daytime hike one weekend.

"We leave at midday," said Jack. "Granddad lives in Stonevale, the railroad town, ten miles down the highway from Greenplains, where we live. He will drive us home long before bedtime. No chance to hitchhike or get on a mailman's truck. Maybe we will need our raincoats."

"We cannot get lost, can we, Jack?" asked Ed.

"No," Jack said. "We go straight from town to some crossroads. I forget myself which way we go from there, but the signs will tell us."

Before long the boys came to the crossroads.

"Jack," cried Ed, "the wind has blown down the sign pole. We cannot tell the way. That sign is useless."

Ed was right. The pole lay on the ground as you see it in the drawing. How should the boys turn it to point the right way? Needless to say, they were upset.

What do you think the boys should do?

Test

10 Cowboy Compounds

moonlight
teaspoon
footprint
jigsaw
cowboy
oilskin
bathroom
outlook
boathouse
outlaw
bookcase
football
faultless
soybean
notebook
sawdust
downtown
topsoil

ⓢ

yourself
throughout

The words in the spelling list are compounds with two-letter vowel sounds.

We spell two-letter vowel sounds in the eye-syllables of compounds as we spell them in one-syllable words.

cow boy   ⎣**cow**˄**boy**⎦

 **1.** Write the compounds with /ou/. Circle the snurk.

43

moon͵light͵

tea͵spoon͵

foot͵print͵

jig͵saw͵

cow͵boy͵

oil͵skin͵

bath͵room͵

out͵look͵

boat͵house͵

out͵law͵

book͵case͵

foot͵ball͵

fault͵less͵

soy͵bean͵

note͵book͵

saw͵dust͵

down͵town͵

top͵soil͵

your͵self͵

through͵out͵

2. Write the compounds with /u̇/ or /ü/.

3. Write the compounds with /oi/.

4. Write compounds that start with these words.

    a. fault   **b.** jig   **c.** your   **d.** saw

Working with the Words

Dictionary Skills

Dictionaries show the pronunciation of each syllable in words with more than one syllable. The word parts we hear are called **ear-syllables.**

throughout /thrü′ out′/

bookcase /bu̇k′ kās′/

1. Write the words with these ear-syllables.

    a. /soi′ bēn′/   **b.** /out′ lu̇k′/   **c.** /bōt′ hous′/

2. Write these picture words.

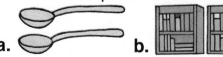

  a.   **b.**   **c.**

Spelling Helps Language

The abbreviation **prep.** stands for **preposition.**

up /up/ *prep.* To a higher place.

1. Write **faultless, throughout, into,** and **yourself.**
   Underline the prepositions. Use the dictionary.

2. **Proofread** the sentences. Find five mistakes and
   write the sentences correctly.

> 1. Cowboys throughout the southwest are
>   sometimes called cowhands.
> 2. At midnight someone heard a horse's
>   hoofbeets.
> 3. Do we eat oatmeal with a teaspoons.
> 4. It isn't hard to make footprints in
>   damp sawdust?

Word Wu??le

noon good

— —

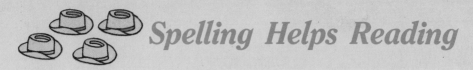

Sound out the words. Then read the story.

sawmill	blowout	footstool	lighthouse	outfit
because	cowhand	fireproof	background	lookout
softball	fallout	household	soundproof	toothbrush

"Here comes Mr. Houseman in his rowboat," said Jenny. "Something must have got in his hen house. He will blame Cowboy."

Mr. Houseman was a farmer who lived downstream southwest of the Baldwin place. For weeks his hen house had been robbed and he was sure Jenny's coonhound, Cowboy, was the outlaw. His booted footsteps came stamping up the footpath to where Jenny was sitting on a footstool in the boathouse.

"It was your coonhound that just got my hen!" shouted the farmer. "I was on the lookout. I gave him a blast of buckshot from my shotgun, but he outran me. Just now he swam to your side. I saw his pawprints—and there he is!"

"Mr. Houseman," said Jenny, hugging the dog. "Cowboy was not in your hen house. I can prove it to you."

How did Jenny prove that Cowboy was not to blame?

Test

11 Airborne Compounds

downstairs
scarecrow
northwest
cartwheel
iceberg
airport
farewell
forenoon
sunburn
eardrum
warehouse
popcorn
cardboard
bluebird
barefoot
landlord
charcoal
birthday
earthquake
reindeer

The words in the spelling list are compounds with vowel-r sounds. We spell vowel-r sounds in the eye-syllables of compounds the same ways we spell them in one-syllable words.

air borne   air borne

1. Write the six compounds with /ãr/ sounds.

2. Write the three compounds with the /är/ sounds.

47

3. Write the six compounds with /ôr/ sounds.

4. Write the compounds that start with these words.

   a. ice   **b.** blue   **c.** birth

   d. sun   **e.** ear   **f.** earth

5. Write the snurks. Circle the word in which **ei** spells /ā/.

Working with the Words

Dictionary Skills

Dictionaries sometimes give a sentence to help show the meaning of an entry word.

forenoon /fôr′nün′/ *n.* Morning; time before noon: *The baseball game was played in the forenoon.*

1. Read the sentences in the Spelling Dictionary for **downstairs** and **farewell.** Write sentences to show the meanings of **charcoal** and **iceberg.**

2. Write these sentences using spelling words.

   a. At the ___ they sell ___ in ___ boxes.

   b. The sun was so hot that I got a ___.

   c. Sacks of black ___ were stored in the ___.

3. These compounds have scrambled word parts. Write the compounds correctly.

earthdeer	**reinbird**	**landwell**
bluedrum	**earlord**	**farequake**

Spelling Helps Language

1. These new compounds have scrambled word parts. Write the compounds correctly.

birdstick	**bookfork**	**pitchmark**
forehouse	**earcast**	**yardring**

down stairs
scare crow
north west
cart wheel
ice berg
air port
fare well
fore noon
sun burn
ear drum
ware house
pop corn
card board
blue bird
bare foot
land lord
char coal
birth day
earth quake
rein deer

The abbreviation **adv.** stands for **adverb.**
An adverb tells things like **when, where,
how much,** and **how.**

downstairs /doun' stãrz'/ *adv.* To a lower floor
in a building: *She ran downstairs.*

2. Find **northwest, nearby, upstairs, cartwheel,** and
forecast in the Spelling Dictionary. Write the
words that can be used as adverbs.

3. Find **farewell, forenoon, sunburn,** and **reindeer** in
the dictionary. Write the words. Underline those
that can be used as nouns.

When we write a person's words, we put
quotation marks around them. We put a
comma between the person's words and
the rest of the sentence.

Pete said, "I like popcorn."

4. Proofread the sentences. Find two spelling
mistakes and two punctuation mistakes in the
sentences. Write the sentences correctly.

Pete said "I like to go barfoot."
That scarcrow is funny," laughed Barb.

Spelling Helps Reading

Sound out the compounds. Then read the story.

herself	pitchfork	deerskin	barnyard	fairgrounds
upstairs	northeast	forecast	haircut	snowstorm
bookmark	birdhouse	farmyard	yardstick	nightmare
earring	airborne	nearby	whirlpool	purse-strings

Mr. Carstairs was the chairman of a firm that made cardboard boxes. On Thursday he found that he could make a big sale in a seaport town in the Northeast. His foreman and workmen were pleased. They bade him farewell and got ready to drive him down the turnpike to the airport.

But as he came downstairs, Carl Forster, the warehouse night watchman, rushed forward.

"Mr. Carstairs, be forewarned! Do not dare get in that airplane! I foresee great harm. The past three nights I have had nightmares. I dreamed your airplane was in a snowstorm and crashed on the outskirts of town."

But carefree Mr. Carstairs did not listen to this outburst. He took the trip and came back on the weekend safe and sound. The first thing he did on Monday was to fire Carl.

Why do you think he fired him?

How many vowel-r compounds are in the story?

Test

field
chief
thief
view
whom
breath
meant
thread
death
health
guard
built
ache
month
glove
tongue
wolf
worm
worth
court

12 Snurk Headaches

We learn to spell snurks by finding their unexpected spellings and remembering them.

1. Say the snurks in the spelling list.
Check the vowel sounds and spellings.

2. Write the snurks that belong in these spaces:

a. The **ie** spells /ī/ in **pie**, but not in ___,
___, ___, and ___.

b. The **ea** spells /ē/ in **clean**, but not in ___,
___, ___, ___, and ___.

c. The **or** spells /ôr/ in **storm,** but not in ___
and ___.

d. The **oo** spells /u̇/ in **book**, but **o** spells /u̇/ in ___.

e. The **ou** spells /ou/ in **loud,** but not in ___.

f. The **u** spells /u/ in **cup,** but **o** spells /u/ in ___,
___, and ___.

3. Write the words with these consonant spellings:

   a. wh spells /h/   **b. ch** spells /k/   **c. gu** spells /g/

4. Write the words with these vowel spellings:

   a. ui spells /i/   **b. o** spells /ü/   **c. iew** spells /ū/

Working with the Words

1. Write the picture snurks.

a.   b.   c.

field
chief
thief
view
whom
breath
meant
thread
death
health
guard
built
ache
month
glove
tongue
wolf
worm
worth
court

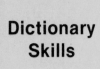

Dictionary Skills

A dictionary sign always stands for the same sound, no matter how the sound is spelled in a word.

/e/ **men** /men/   **meant** /ment/

/i/ **hill** /hil/   **built** /bilt/

2. Write the words with these sounds:

  a. /ē/

  b. /u/

3. Write these sentences using a snurk to fill each space. Punctuate the sentences correctly.

  a. One who steals is a ____

  b. The head of a tribe is a ____

  c. A piece of land with few trees is a ____

  d. What is in your sight is a ____

  e. Do ____ keep your hands warm

4. Write a sentence in which someone tells a doctor about a toothache. Use **said, to, have,** and the abbreviation for **Doctor.** Use quotation marks and commas correctly.

54

Spelling Helps Language

> The abbreviation **pron.** stands for **pronoun,** a word that is used in place of a noun. Words like **they, we, I,** and **him** are pronouns.
>
> **you** /ū/ *pron.* The one being spoken to: *This gift is for you.*

1. Unscramble the words to tell what Jim said. Underline the pronouns.

> bread   you   want   give   I   to   some

2. Proofread these sentences to find four mistakes. Write the sentences correctly.

> 1. "Give the password" cried the guard.
> 2. She is the one for whom I work.
> 3. I wood like a bowl of soup.
> 4. There are six horses in the feild," said Dr. Goldstone.

Word Wu??le

Gloves   Gloves

a __ of __

Spelling Helps Reading

Say the snurks.

who	fought	word	your	child	gone	wear
shoe	thought	work	want	rough	love	earn
ought	could	there	weigh	tough	done	learn
bought	would	bread	weight	live	none	won
brought	should	head	eight	give	one	son

Complete the sentences.

1. **Baseball** is to **field** as **basketball** is to...
    a. street   **b.** court   **c.** soup

2. **Leader** is to **group** as **chief** is to...
    a. tribe   **b.** team   **c.** wolf

3. **Week** is to **month** as **month** is to...
    a. day   **b.** year   **c.** midnight

4. **Tongue** is to **mouth** as **hand** is to...
    a. head   **b.** walk   **c.** glove

5. **Mean** is to **meant** as **build** is to...
    a. bought   **b.** built   **c.** fought

I do not mind a snurk or two,
Though I won't ever love them,
But twenty snurks a week, I say,
Is just too many of them!

Test

13 One O'clock Contractions

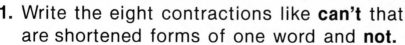

A **contraction** is one word or a put-together word that is shortened by leaving out one or more letters. We use an **apostrophe** in place of the missing letters.

he is	he's	we are	we're

 1. Write the eight contractions like **can't** that are shortened forms of one word and **not**.

2. Write the six contractions like **she's** that are shortened forms of one word and **is.**

aren't
doesn't
weren't
wasn't
shouldn't
wouldn't
hadn't
hasn't
we're
ma'am
there's
that's
where's
who's
what's
he's
they've
you've
they'll
she'll

aren't
doesn't
weren't
wasn't
shouldn't
wouldn't
hadn't
hasn't
we're
ma'am
there's
that's
where's
who's
what's
he's
they've
you've
they'll
she'll

3. Write the contractions like **we'll** that are shortened forms of one word and **will** or **shall**.

4. Write the contractions for **you have, they have, we are,** and **madam.**

Working with the Words

Dictionary Skills

Dictionaries show contractions as entry words.

ma'am /mam/ *n.* Madam; a title used to address a woman: *"I have a letter for you, ma'am,"* said the mail clerk.

1. Write these contractions from left to right in the order they come as entries in the Spelling Dictionary: **wouldn't, weren't, wasn't, we're, what's,** and **who's.**

2. Write the meanings of these contractions.

    a. doesn't   **b.** what's   **c.** they've

Homonyms are words that sound alike, but have different meanings and spellings.
there: I live **there.**
their: That's **their** new house.
they're: **They're** in my class at school.

58

3. Write the sentences. Use contractions for the spaces.

   a. ___ a car in the driveway that looks like theirs.

   b. ___ going to tell me whose book this is?

4. Use **your** and the review contraction for **you are** in the first sentence. Use **its** and the review contraction for **it is** in the second sentence.

   a. I think ___ proud of ___ new outfit, aren't you?

   b. ___ too bad that the bird hurt ___ wing.

Word Wu??le

Who Who
_____
First

___ *on* ___ ?

The abbreviation **etc.** stands for **et cetera,** the Latin words for "and other things." We use commas between the words in the list including **etc.**

I have pins, pens, clips, etc.

1. Write the meaning the dictionary gives for **etc.**

An **apostrophe** in a contraction stands for missing letters.

An **apostrophe** with **s** shows possession, or belonging.

Ann's bike   **Joe's foot**   **the car's tire**

2. Write the underlined words in a shortened way by using an apostrophe to show possession.

The fur of the cat stood on end.

3. Proofread the sentences and write them correctly.

> 1. Jeff's popcorn wouldnt pop.
> 2. Ill help you if youll let me.
> 3. Get me nails, paint, wood etc.

Read the contractions. Then read the story.

can't	I'd	you'd	they'd	we'll	we've	won't
couldn't	o'clock	she's	isn't	he'll	don't	I've
here's	she'd	who'll	he'd	let's	I'm	haven't

"We're through with our work, aren't we, Miss White?" asked Dick. "Let's ask Jane if she doesn't have a good trick for our class. She'll have a good one, I'm sure."

"That's true. You've done well," said Miss White. "What's your trick, Jane?"

"Well, ma'am," said Jane, "they've stacked six books side by side. Each book is two inches thick and has 200 pages. There's a bookworm who's going to chew from Page 1 in Book 1 to Page 200 in Book 6. We shouldn't count the covers. How many pages did the bookworm eat through? How many inches did he go?"

"That wasn't tough!" cried Dick. "He ate through 12 inches and 1,200 pages."

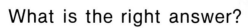

"I wouldn't be so quick," smiled Jane. "You weren't right, Dick. Think! Where's Page 1 in Book 1? And where's page 200 in Book 6?"

What is the right answer?

Test

61

battle
paddle
puddle
kettle
simple
rifle
ankle
stumble
sprinkle
eagle
model
label
level
nickel
petal
medal
total
metal
❧ *couple*
❧ *trouble*

14 Rival Noodle Quarrel

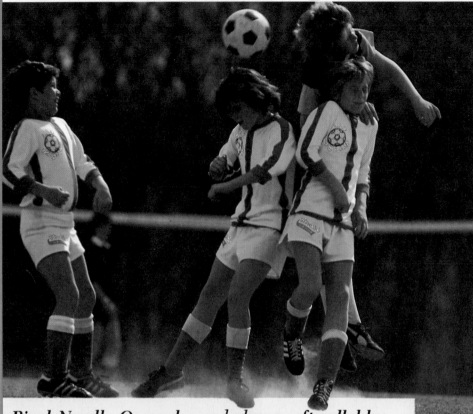

*Rival Noodle Quarrel words have **soft-syllable endings** that sound alike.*
We show the soft-syllable endings like this: /əl/.
We spell the /əl/ endings like this:

> **al** in words like **rival**
>
> **le** in words like **noodle**
>
> **el** in words like **quarrel**

 1. Write the twelve **le**-ending words. Underline the word that means "trip and fall."

2. Write the four **al**-ending words.
Circle the word that means "the sum."

3. Write the four **el**-ending words.
Circle the word that means "flat."

4. Write the picture words.

a.   b.    c.

Working with the Words

Dictionary Skills

The **schwa /ə/** shows the vowel sound in a soft syllable when the vowel sound is not plain and clear.

1. Write the /əl/ picture words.

a.   b.    c.

2. Write the words with these sounds.

   /ē/   /ō/   /ī/

3. Find **trouble, simple,** and **petal** in the Spelling Dictionary. Write the word that is used as a noun <u>and</u> as a verb.

63

Spelling Helps Language

Synonyms are words with the same meaning, or nearly the same meaning.
Antonyms are words with opposite meanings.
   syn. is the abbreviation for **synonym.**
   ant. is the abbreviation for **antonym.**

1. Use nine words from the box to write a synonym for each /əl/-ending word below.

stone	shake	scare	pain	hang
fine	fall	sum	name	two

a. title   **b.** couple   **c.** dangle

d. total   **e.** rattle   **f.** startle

g. pebble   **h.** stumble   **i.** noble

2. Use words from the box to write the antonyms.

hard	rising	sob

a. giggle   **b.** simple   **c.** setting

Word Wu??le

keTtle

a __ __

When a person's words form a question, we put a **question mark** inside the quotation marks.

"Did you sprain your ankle?" asked Ethel.

3. Write sentences using the questions in the speech balloons. Have the sentences end with **he asked, she asked,** and **asked Don.**

Will they be trouble to take care of?

Are those dogs poodles?

Would you like to have a couple of pups?

bat tle
pad dle
pud dle
ket tle
sim ple
ri fle
an kle
stum ble
sprin kle
ea gle
mod el
la bel
lev el
nick el
pet al
med al
to tal
met al
coup le
troub le

4. Proofread this sentence. Write it correctly.

"Do **stumble, levle, tremble,** and **tumble** have the same meaning," asked Ann with a twinkel in her eye.

Spelling Helps Reading

Sound out the words.

scramble	noble	twinkle	oval	freckle	plural
travel	stable	local	marble	mumble	title
camel	tremble	shuffle	settle	noodle	sandal

Choose the word in each row that does not belong.

1. single   pencil   double   triple
2. brutal   noble   loyal   gentle
3. poodle   beagle   mongrel   camel
4. tackle   dribble   oral   hurdle
5. signal   muddle   fumble   tangle
6. battle   travel   struggle   quarrel
7. marble   pebble   gravel   flannel
8. dazzle   sparkle   sprinkle   twinkle

Metal kettle? Maple table?
Nickel pickle? Staple label?
Poodle doodle? Camel saddle?
Sandal handle? Naval battle?
Total muddle? Triple trouble?
l-e, a-l, or **e-l?**
Soft syllables, you're hard to spell!

Test

15 Minor Dinner Burglars

Minor, Dinner, and **Burglar** words have **soft-syllable endings** that sound alike.
We show the ending sounds like this: /ər/.
We spell the /ər/ endings like this:

> **er** in words like **dinner**

> **or** in words like **minor**

> **ar** in words like **burglar**

bother
whether
daughter
farther
quarter
offer
rather
author
motor
humor
tractor
favor
flavor
razor
dollar
burglar
danger
shoulder
neither
either

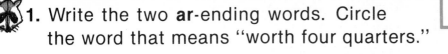

1. Write the two **ar**-ending words. Circle the word that means "worth four quarters."

both er
wheth er
daugh ter
far ther
quar ter
of fer
rath er
au thor
mo tor
hu mor
trac tor
fa vor
fla vor
ra zor
dol lar
bur glar
dan ger
shoul der
nei ther
ei ther

2. Write the seven **or** words. Circle the word that means "taste."

3. Write the eleven **er** words. Circle the synonym for **trouble.**

4. Write the picture words.

a.   **b.**   **c.**

d.   **e.**   **f.**

Working with the Words

Dictionary Skills

Dictionaries show two ways to pronounce **either** and **neither.**

either /ē′ ᴛʜər/ or /ī′ ᴛʜər/

neither /nē′ ᴛʜər/ or /nī′ ᴛʜər/

1. Write **either** and **neither.** Beside each word, show the pronunciation you would rather use.

2. Write the words that start with /sh/, /hw/, or /ô/. In each word, underline the letters that spell /ər/.

3. Write the sentences with spelling words.

a. He doesn't know ___ his ___ can go much ___.

b. His ___ is glad she can sit on his ___.

c. The ___ must have put a lot of ___ in the book.

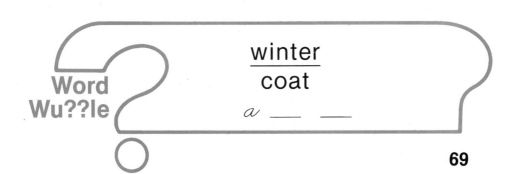

Word Wu??le

winter
coat

a ___ ___

Spelling Helps Language

The abbreviation **no.** stands for **number,** as in **no. 7.** We also use **No.** for **North,** as in **No. River Road.** Another abbreviation for **North** is **N.,** as in **N.C.** or **NC** (North Carolina) and **N.D.** or **ND** (North Dakota).

1. Write the plural forms of **no., Dr., doctor,** and **number.** Use the Spelling Dictionary.

2. Add **er** to these words to write more /ər/ words. By each word, write **n.** for **noun** or **adj.** for **adjective.**

new	old	roost	bright	board

3. Proofread the sentences and write them correctly. Mark each sentence **True** or **False.**

> 1. A quarter is worth less than one doller.
> 2. Your head is above you're sholders.
> 3. My brothers daughter is my sister.
> 4. Eagels and jays can fly.

Spelling Helps Reading

Sound out the words. Then read the story.

rooster	eager	anchor	power	grammar	mister
sailor	minor	drawer	mayor	harbor	whisker
trouser	scatter	mirror	bitter	further	litter
painter	partner	ruler	collar	order	lumber

"Bess," said Mrs. Beecher to her daughter, "you and your brother Victor better march down to Mr. Taylor's barbershop. Look in that mirror! Neither of you has seen a clipper on your head for months. Be back in time for dinner."

She gave the twins ten dollars. Off they scampered. Mr. Taylor was in a good humor.

"The Beecher twins!" he cried. "Shall I get out my razor and lather and shave off your whiskers, Victor?"

"Don't bother, Mr. Taylor," smiled Victor. "I'd rather have a haircut."

"Your father tells me you're clever with numbers," said Mr. Taylor. "Teachers give you good grades? Now, I never make an error. Say, how many Beecher kids are there?"

"Well," grinned Victor, "I have as many brothers as sisters."

"And I have twice as many brothers as sisters," said Bess. "So you can tell how many Beecher kids there are."

How many Beecher kids can you count?

Test

supply
reply
copy
county
jelly
clumsy
duty
windy
crazy
lady
noisy
lonely
cooky
envy
greedy
navy
pity
bury
marry
worry

16 **Noisy July Words**

*Each word in the spelling list is a two-syllable word that ends in **y**. The final **y** spells /ī/ when the last syllable is accented.*

July /jə lī′/

*The final **y** spells /ē/ when the last syllable is an unaccented, or soft, syllable.*

noisy /noi′ zē/

1. Say the spelling words. Hear /ī/ in **reply** and **supply.** Hear /ē/ in all of the other words.

2. Write the words in which the last syllable is accented.

3. Write the snurks. Circle the word that means "wed."

4. Write the words that start with /k/, /d/, or /g/.

5. Write the four words that start with /n/ or /l/. Underline the antonym of **quiet.**

6. Write **envy, pity, windy,** and **jelly.** Underline the word that comes before the others in the dictionary.

> When a noun ends in a **consonant** and **y,** we change **y** to **i** and add **es** to spell the plural form.
>
> baby—babies   reply—replies

7. Write the plural forms of **supply, lady,** and **county.**

 Working with the Words

> When a verb ends in a **consonant** and **y,** we change **y** to **i** before adding **ed** or **es**—but not before **ing.**
>
> copy—copies—copied—copying

1. Write the **es, ed,** and **ing** forms of these verbs:

a. bury   **b.** envy

Word list
sup ply
re ply
cop y
coun ty
jel ly
clum sy
du ty
win dy
cra zy
la dy
noi sy
lone ly
cook y
en vy
greed y
na vy
pit y
bur y
mar ry
wor ry

2. Write the sentences using the plural of **lady** and **cooky** and the **ed** forms of **pity** and **supply**.

a. Two kind ___ ___ the starving pony.

b. He has ___ them with lots of ___.

> When an adjective ends in a **consonant** and **y**, we change **y** to **i** before we add **er** or **est**.
>
> greedy — greedier — greediest

3. Add **er** and **est** to **greedy**, **lonely**, and **clumsy**.

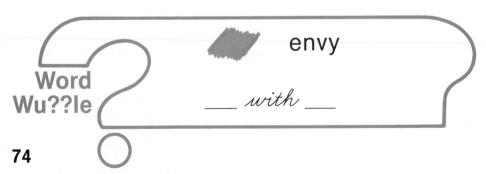

Word Wu??le

envy

___ *with* ___

Spelling Helps Language

Co. is the abbreviation for **County** and for **Company** as in this sentence:
  Send the bill to **Fox Candy Co.,**
  in **Cole Co., Texas.**
We do not use **Co.** in sentences like this:
  Mr. Fox owns a candy **company** in this **county.**

1. Find **dizzy, cozy,** and **jelly** in the dictionary. Write the words for which **er** and **est** forms are shown.

2. Find **marry, duty,** and **pity** in the dictionary. Write the words for which the **ed** form is shown.

3. **Proofread** this note to find four mistakes. Write the note correctly.

Dear Girls,
  I'm worried. We need a bigger supply of jelly cookys. It's a pity we dont have two dollers to spend. What shall we do. Please reply.
        Sandy

Spelling Helps Reading

plenty	dizzy	safety	shiny	truly	twenty	shady
buggy	speedy	smoky	simply	sturdy	thirty	fifty
cozy	gently	foggy	jolly	dairy	forty	ninety

"Class," said Miss White, "you've done mighty well with your school work. Tidy up those messy desks. If Jane has one of her riddles ready, we'll be happy to hear it."

"Good!" cried Billy. "Brainy Jane has dandy puzzles. Riddles are her hobby. Give us a tricky one, Jane!"

"Very well," said Jane. "A mother duck had a noisy flock of ducklings. One sunny day they were hungry and thirsty, so she told them to march down to the pond. The frisky little ones were so greedy they could hardly wait.

"'This is the way you will march,' said the fussy mother duck sternly. 'One duckling will march in front of two ducklings. One will march in the middle of two ducklings. One will march in back of two. Step lively, now!'

"The clumsy little ones marched down the sandy path on their stubby little legs. Now the puzzle is, how many ducklings were in the flock?"

"Easy," cried Nancy. "Nine!"

"No, Smarty," cried Denny. "There were five!"

Well, how many were there?

Test

17 Center Circle Words

slice
price
juice
choice
scarce
ounce
center
circle
cigar
fancy
cave
code
cub
cure
crop
club
cattle
copper
fierce
once

We use c to spell /k/ before **a, o, u,** and **consonant letters.**

We use c to spell /s/ before **e, i,** and **y.**

1. Say the words. Hear the /s/ and /k/ sounds.

2. Write the eight words that start with /k/. Underline the word that names a metal.

3. Write the words that have the /k/ sound, but do not start with /k/. Underline the word that means "hard to get."

4. Write the five words that start with /s/.
Underline the word that means "the middle place."

5. Write the words that end with **ce**. Underline /wuns/.

6. Write the six two-syllable words.
Underline the antonym of **plain.**

Working with the Words

Dictionary Skills

Some words have more than one meaning, or definition. Dictionaries number the meanings.

club /klub/ *n.* **1.** Heavy stick used as a weapon. **2.** Stick used to hit a ball in some games: *golf club.* **3.** Group of people joined for a purpose. —*v.* Beat or hit with a club. **clubbed, clubbing.**

1. Write the words that start with /k/. After each word write the number of noun definitions the Spelling Dictionary shows.

2. Write the words that end with /əl/ or /ər/.

3. Write **cigar, fancy,** and **choice.** Circle the word in which you hear /ə/ in the soft syllable.

4. Write these questions with correct punctuation. Use words, or their plural forms, from the list to fill the spaces.

a. What is the ___ of eight ___ of grape ___

b. Is a bear ___ when she is in her ___ with her ___

Spelling Helps Language

The abbreviation for **ounce** is **oz.** People think that the abbreviation was once an **o.** Long ago printers sometimes put a curved mark after abbreviations as we now use periods. The printer's mark looked like the letter **z,** so people began to spell the abbreviation **oz.**

1. Find **ounce** and **oz.** in the Spelling Dictionary Write the plural forms.

slice
price
juice
choice
scarce
ounce
cen₁ter
cir₁cle
ci₁gar
fan₁cy
cave
code
cub
cure
crop
club
cat₁tle
cop₁per
fierce
once

79

2. Use **brace, scarce,** and **glance** to write synonyms.

   a. prop   **b.** look   **c.** rare

3. Proofread the letter and write it correctly.

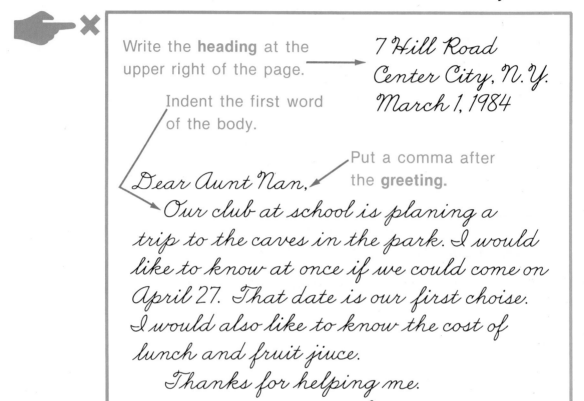

Write the **heading** at the upper right of the page. →

7 Hill Road
Center City, N.Y.
March 1, 1984

Indent the first word of the body.

Put a comma after the **greeting.**

Dear Aunt Nan,
    Our club at school is planing a trip to the caves in the park. I would like to know at once if we could come on April 27. That date is our first choise. I would also like to know the cost of lunch and fruit jiuce.
    Thanks for helping me.
              Love,
              Grace

Put a comma after the **complimentary close.**

Word Wu??le

face
face friend

___ ___ ___

Sound out the words. Read the verse aloud.

rice	cent	peace	mice	fence	place	since
trace	cell	cinder	cider	dance	face	twice
cedar	glance	cellar	icy	juicy	cities	lacy

Girls: Make up your mind, you two-faced **C**!
Choose s or k. Which will you be?
In front of **a** and **o** and **u**
You spell the **k** sound. Yes, you do!
In front of **e** and **i** and **y**
You act like s. Please tell us why.

Boys: You sound like s in **nice** and **mice**,
In **rice** and **twice** and **price** and **slice**.
You show your **face** in **lace** and **race**,
In **brace** and **grace** and **trace** and **place**.
Why not show up in **base** and **vase**?
And why an s in **case** and **chase**?

All: You goof off when we must spell **rinse**,
But back you come in **since** and **prince**.
And worst of all the things we've heard,
You'll spell both sounds within one word!
Our trust is gone! Our hopes are spent!
—See **circle**, **scarce**, and **accident**.

Test

dumb
limb
knit
kneel
knight
wren
wreck
answer
sword
listen
often
castle
whistle
wrestle
honor
honest
doubt
island
☜sign
☜ghost

18 Listen Words

The **Listen** words have
silent-consonant letters.
A **silent-consonant letter** is one that
does not spell a sound in a word.

listen /lis′ ən/

1. Write **sign, doubt, island,** and **knight.** Underline each consonant that spells a sound.

2. Write  , 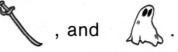 , and .

3. Use words from the spelling list to fill the spaces.

a. b spells /b/ in **bother** and **trouble,** but not after **m** in ___ and ___.

b. k spells /k/ in **king** and **ankle,** but not before **n** in ___, ___, and ___.

c. w spells /w/ in **week,** but not before **r** in ___, ___, and ___.

d. w spells /w/ in **worm,** but not after **s** in ___ and ___.

e. h spells /h/ in **house,** but **h** is silent in ___, ___, and ___.

f. t spells /t/ in **tractor** and **print,** but **t** is silent in ___, ___, ___, ___, and ___.

Working with the Words

Dictionary Skills	Dictionary sound-spelling does not show silent letters.

knight /nīt/   **castle** /kas′ əl/

1. Write the spelling words for which the Spelling Dictionary shows these pronunciations.

a. /nēl/   **b.** /kas′ əl/   **c.** /ī′ lənd/

d. /rek/   **e.** /sīn/   **f.** /lis′ ən/

dumb
limb
knit
kneel
knight
wren
wreck
answer
sword
listen
often
castle
whistle
wrestle
honor
honest
doubt
island
sign
ghost

2. Write the picture words.

a.   b.   c.

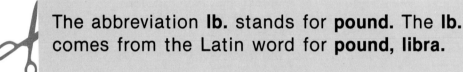

Spelling Helps Language

The abbreviation **lb.** stands for **pound**. The **lb.** comes from the Latin word for **pound, libra.**

1. Write the plural forms of **ghost, sign, lb.,** and **answer.** Use the Spelling Dictionary.

2. Proofread the words to find any that cannot be used as nouns. Write the lists correctly.

1. island, kneel, cattle, ghost
2. sword, cigar, often, wren
3. listen, limb, tongue, castle
4. cent, copper, dumb, health

Word Wu??le

THUMB

a __ __

Sound out the words.

trestle	wrench	wrinkle	knee	soften	daughter
wrap	write	thumb	knuckle	hour	straight
wrist	wreath	knob	glisten	taught	knot

Read the sentences. Explain what each sentence really means.

1. If you can't stand the heat, get out of the kitchen.
2. The pen is mightier than the sword.
3. A soft answer turns away wrath.
4. She is haunted by ghosts of her past.
5. He's a wolf in lamb's clothing.
6. Honest men are as scarce as hens' teeth.
7. Don't switch horses in midstream.
8. Don't cross that bridge before you come to it.
9. Half a loaf is better than none.
10. Two wrongs don't make a right.
11. Don't fasten the barn door after the horses are stolen.
12. Talk is cheap.

Dictionaries show **wh** words like **wheel** as /hwēl/. Many people have stopped using the /h/ and now say /wēl/ instead.

Test

19 Pedal Peddle Homonyms

beet
beat
its
it's
groan
grown
hall
haul
mail
male
pane
pain
plain
plane
pedal
peddle
root
route
wait
weight

Homonyms *are words that sound alike but have different meanings and different spellings.*

pedal /ped′ əl/ *v.* Work the pedals of.

peddle /ped′ əl/ *v.* Carry from place to place and sell.

 1. Say the homonyms. Use the Spelling Dictionary to make sure of the meanings.

2. Write the words for the meanings. Under them, write their homonyms.

    a. hit   **b.** drag   **c.** it is

3. Write the words for the meanings.
Under them, write their homonyms.

    a. moan   **b.** an ache   **c.** a way to go

    d. pause   **e.** not fancy   **f.** carry about to sell

4. Write the /ā/ words. Underline the word that means "man or boy." Circle the snurk.

Working with the Words

Dictionary Skills

Some words with the same spelling have different meanings. Dictionaries show both words as entry words with numbers. Words with the same spelling and different meanings are **homographs.**

root[1] /rüt/ *n.* Part of a plant from which the plant grows.

root[2] /rüt/ *v.* Cheer for a team.

1. Write both /rüt/ spelling words.
Circle the word that would likely be on a map.

2. Write **pane, beet, groan,** and **plane.** Underline the word which has two entries in the dictionary.

beet
beat
its
it's
groan
grown
hall
haul
mail
male
pane
pain
plain
plane
ped‚al
ped‚dle
root
route
wait
weight

3. Write the picture words.
Under them, write their homonyms.

a.  b.  c.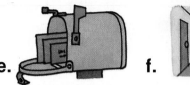

d. e. f.

4. Write the sentences correctly using words
from the spelling list.

a. does a dog wag ___ tail when ___ happy

b. many peddlers use this ___ when
they ___ their goods.

5. Write the sentences with words from the spelling
list. Put in the missing **exclamation marks** (!).

a. I'm coming ___ for me

b. What a ___ I have in my right ankle

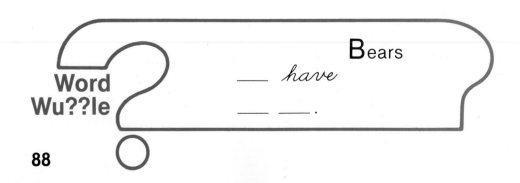

**Word
Wu??le**

___ *have* **B**ears

___ ___ .

Spelling Helps Language

The abbreviation for **Road** is **Rd.** This abbreviation is never used alone. It is always used with the name of a street, as when we say **Shore Rd.** or **South County Rd.** or **207 Blake Rd.**

1. Write your own sentence using the homonyms **rode** and **road** and the abbreviation **rd.**

2. There are thirteen sets of review homonyms on page 90. Use nine words from the list to write antonyms for these words.

   a. sell   **b.** fix   **c.** wrong

   d. lost   **e.** old   **f.** wouldn't

   g. there   **h.** from   **i.** here

3. Use words from the sets of review homonyms on page 90 to fill the spaces. Remember: Each word must fit with the other three words in the row.

a. deer	horse	fox	___
b. two	one	four	___
c. your	our	her	___
d. see	smell	feel	___
e. blue	yellow	green	___

89

Spelling Helps Reading

Say the words.

by	ate	write	break	bare	their	to
buy	eight	right	brake	bear	there	two
						too

read	one	here	knew	know	would
red	won	hear	new	no	wood

 **Proofread** the sentences and write them correctly.

1. Its too late for the bird to lay it's eggs.
2. It's plain to see that the plane can't land here.
3. The roots of the beets grew from two to four inches deep.
4. I know that their is no better route to the city.
5. A full-grown male tiger may reach a weight of 400 pounds.
6. Don't wait till the pane in your arm makes you groan.
7. We raise beats and haul them too town to sell there.
8. The pedal and brake on my bike would have to be fixed.
9. We will have to hall the mail to the airport ourselves.
10. We knew we would hear from our deer friends right soon.

Some people pronounce **route** like this: /rüt/.
Some people pronounce **route** like this: /rout/.

Test

20 Sore Toe Homonyms

Homonyms are words that sound alike but have different spellings and different meanings.

pare /pãr/ *v.* Peel.

pair /pãr/ *n.* Two of a kind.

pear /pãr/ *n.* A kind of fruit.

 1. Write the words for the meanings.
Under them, write their homonyms.

a. take a quick look

b. pull by a rope

c. make poor use of

peek
peak
scene
seen
steel
steal
tide
tied
shown
shone
sore
soar
peace
piece
tow
toe
waist
waste
pare
pair
pear

91

peek
peak
scene
seen
steel
steal
tide
tied
shown
shone
sore
soar
peace
piece
tow
toe
waist
waste
pare
pair
pear

2. Write the words for the meanings.
Under them, write their homonyms.

a. a view   **b.** twinkled   **c.** fly high

d. take what   **e.** part of a   **f.** fastened with
    is not yours   whole thing   rope or string

3. Write and its homonyms. Underline the
word that means "peel."

 Working with the Words

Dictionary Skills

When verb forms are <u>regular</u> like
walk, (have) **walked, walking,**
dictionaries do not show
the different verb forms.

When verbs are <u>not regular</u>,
dictionaries show the different
forms.

steal /stēl/ *v.* Rob; take away.
stole, stolen, stealing.

1. Write **steal—stole, show—shown,** and
shine—shone. Circle the "past" words.

2. Write the snurks. Circle the word pronounced /pēs/.

3. Complete the sentences with homonyms from the spelling list and the Spelling Helps Reading list.

   a. Have you ___ a tight ___ in the rope?

   b. Don't ___ your boat when the ___ is high.

Spelling Helps Language

St. is the abbreviation for **Street** and for **Saint.** The abbreviation **St.** starts with a capital letter because it is always used with a name.

I live at **27 Main St., St. Paul,** Maine.

1. Write two sentences about J. M. Reed who lives on **Gray Street** in **Saint Clair,** a town in your state. Use three abbreviations plus your state abbreviation.

2. Write **road, street, saint, stair, hour,** and **so.** Underline the words that have homonyms.

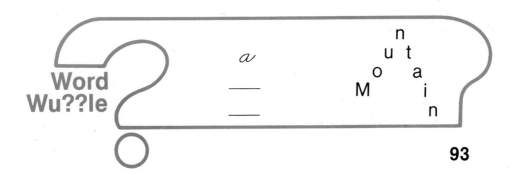

Word Wu??le

a
___
___

n
u t
o   a
M i
n

Spelling Helps Reading

Say the homonyms.

heard	lead	rain	way	tail	sea	sun
herd	led	rein	weigh	tale	see	son
hole	made	road	so	threw	knot	pail
whole	maid	rode	sew	through	not	pale
hour	meat	sail	stair	forth	weak	your
our	meet	sale	stare	fourth	week	you're

Proofread the sentences and write them correctly.

1. We saw a lovely scene from the peak of the hill.
2. I tied up my soar toe with a piece of white cloth.
3. It took a whole hour to pare the peaches and pears.
4. The men had to tow the steal rails down the rode.
5. The sea tide brought the water up to our waists.
6. A pair of hawks sored through the clouds.
7. We should find a way to make peace.
8. We were shone how we had wasted our time.
9. She was seen peeking through a whole in the fence.
10. Lead weighs more than steel.
11. We'll have to wait a weak to sale our boat.
12. A heard of cows came down the dusty rode.

Test

94

21 Traffic Signal Words

collect
correct
account
gallon
announce
success
arrest
accept
traffic
afford
perfect
escape
disturb
signal
argue
admit
object
suspect
◊ comfort
◊ only

Many two-syllable words have a
Vowel-**C**onsonant-**C**onsonant-**V**owel pattern.
Break the **VCCV** words into eye-syllables
between the consonant letters.

traf͵fic,
VC↑CV

sig͵nal,
VC↑CV

Spell each eye-syllable as you spell an
accented one-syllable word.
But always say the whole word by ear-syllables.

 1. Write the ten words with doubled-consonant
letters in the VCCV letter pattern.

2. Write the ten VCCV words that do not have doubled-consonant letters. Circle the snurks.

3. Write the words for the meanings.

    a. get free   **b.** bother   **c.** four quarts

    d. take   **e.** gather   **f.** without faults

Working with the Words

Dictionary Skills

The words **object** and **suspect** each have two pronunciations.

object /ŏb′ jəkt/ *n.* Thing: *A baseball is a round object.* /əb jĕct′/ —*v.* Show dislike: *He objects to noise.*

suspect /səs pĕkt′/ *v.* Think something to be so. /sŭs′ pĕkt/ —*n.* Person suspected.

1. Write the sentences. Underline the loud syllables in **object** and **suspect** in both sentences.

    a. I suspect that the object has been lost.

    b. The suspect did not object to telling his story.

The vowel sound in many soft syllables is hard to hear. Dictionaries show the hard-to-hear vowel sound with /ə/ no matter how it is spelled.

2. Write the VCCV words with these pronunciations:

    a. /ə nouns'/   **b.** /sək ses'/   **c.** /kum' fərt/

3. Write the eye-syllables of each word. Then <u>say</u> the whole word by ear-syllables.

	Eye-Syllables	Ear-Syllables
a. col lect	＿＿ / ＿＿ /	/kə lekt'/
b. cor rect	＿＿ / ＿＿ /	/kə rekt'/
c. ac cept	＿＿ / ＿＿ /	/ak sept'/
d. ac count	＿＿ / ＿＿ /	/ə kount'/
e. dis turb	＿＿ / ＿＿ /	/dis tėrb'/
f. ad mit	＿＿ / ＿＿ /	/ad mit'/
g. es cape	＿＿ / ＿＿ /	/ə skāp'/
h. per fect	＿＿ / ＿＿ /	/pėr' fəkt/

col lect
cor rect
ac count
gal lon
an nounce
suc cess
ar rest
ac cept
traf fic
af ford
per fect
es cape
dis turb
sig nal
ar gue
ad mit
ob ject
sus pect
com fort
on ly

Word Wu??le

S e n t e n c e

a ＿ ＿ ＿

Spelling Helps Language

Blvd. is the abbreviation for **Boulevard.**
Ave. is the abbreviation for **Avenue.**
A **boulevard** is a wide, important city street.
An **avenue** is a street in a city or town.
Both **Blvd.** and **Ave.** are always used with
names and always begin with capital letters.

1. Write a synonym for each word or abbreviation.
   Use words you have learned in the lessons and
   words from the Spelling Helps Reading list on
   page 99.

   a. prop   **b.** Blvd.   **c.** nearly

   d. take   **e.** box   **f.** model

   g. bother   **h.** bloom   **i.** thing

2. **Proofread** the story Carlos wrote for the school
   newspaper. Write the story correctly.

> Our class was desturbed today when a
> a driver was arrested in front of school for
> speeding We could here him arguing and
> objecting before admitting that his traffic
> ticket was fair. As he drove off, Miss Burton
> announced our next lesson. What do you suppose
> the lesson was? A safety lesson!

Sound out the words. Then read the story.

blizzard	lantern	almost	attend	contest	mistake
sentence	insist	support	carton	surround	cannon
blossom	organ	stubborn	pattern	succeed	basket

As was his custom, crabby old Mr. Gannon went to the coffee shop on the corner. He sat at a sidewalk table so he could observe the traffic in comfort. He waved his napkin to signal a waiter. The waiters did not like to serve Mr. Gannon. Though he could afford to, the selfish old fellow never gave tips to the waiters.

"Black coffee and one lump of sugar," he commanded.

The waiter brought the plastic carton of coffee. Mr. Gannon put in the sugar and started to stir. Then he stared at the coffee in horror.

"Sir," he announced, "there is an insect floating in my coffee. I will not accept it. No excuses. I insist on new coffee. Don't argue with me!"

The stubborn waiter snatched the carton on the table and was back in a flash. He set the carton on the table and glared at Mr. Gannon. Mr. Gannon leaned forward and tasted his coffee.

"Rascal!" he roared. "You brought back the same coffee!"

How could Mr. Gannon tell it was the same coffee?

 *Test*

22 Picture Album Words

bargain
excuse
lumber
except
circus
forward
selfish
picnic
subject
platform
market
engine
mistake
carpet
rescue
admire
perhaps
furnace
 welcome
 early

The words in the list have the
Vowel-Consonant-Consonant-Vowel pattern.
Break the **VCCV** words into eye-syllables
between the consonant letters.

pic ˌture	al ˌbum
VC ↑ CV	VC ↑ CV

*Spell each eye-syllable as you spell an
accented one-syllable word.
But always say the whole word by ear-syllables.*

1. Write **engine, admire,** and two snurks. Underline
the word in which **g** spells /j/.

2. Write the words that start with these sounds.

/b/	/l/	/r/
/e/	/e/	/e/
/p/	/p/	/p/

3. Write the words that start with these sounds.

/f/	/f/	/k/
/èr/	/w/	/a/
/s/	/s/	/s/

4. Write **market, mistake, rescue,** and **perhaps.**
Circle the /ā/ word.

Working with the Words

Dictionary Skills

The word **subject** is used as both a <u>noun</u> and a <u>verb</u>.

We say /sub′ jəkt/ for the noun:
The **subject** of my talk is "Flying Objects."

We say /sub jekt′/ for the verb:
Don't **subject** me to so much noise, please.

1. Find **subject, excuse, perhaps,** and **platform** in the Spelling Dictionary. Write the two words that are used as both nouns and verbs.

bar gain
ex cuse
lum ber
ex cept
cir cus
for ward
sel fish
pic nic
sub ject
plat form
mar ket
en gine
mis take
car pet
res cue
ad mire
per haps
fur nace
wel come
ear ly

2. Find **picnic, excuse,** and **rescue** in the dictionary. Write the **ed** and **ing** forms of **picnic, excuse,** and **rescue.**

3. Write the eye-syllables of each word. As you write each eye-syllable, say and spell it like a one-syllable word. Say the whole word by ear-syllables.

	Eye-Syllables	Ear-Syllables
a. market	_____ / _____ /	/mär′ kət/
b. furnace	_____ / _____ /	/fėr′ nəs/
c. lumber	_____ / _____ /	/lum′ bər/
d. engine	_____ / _____ /	/en′ jən/
e. forward	_____ / _____ /	/fôr′ wərd/

Spelling Helps Language

The abbreviation for **gallon** is **gal.**
The abbreviation for **gallons** is **gal.** or **gals.**
We use the abbreviation **gal.** on price tags, on signs, on bills, etc. We do not use it in a sentence like this:

Three **gallons** of milk will cost $3.90.

1. Write a sentence telling how many pints of milk are in a gallon. Use the Spelling Dictionary.

102

2. Use ⟍VC⟍CV⟋ words from the spelling list or Spelling Helps Reading list on page 104 to write synonyms for these words:

a. banner   **b.** whole

c. stage   **d.** act

3. Unscramble the underlined words to write the sentence.

The firefighters in <u>poor the rescued</u> Engine Co. 7 have <u>frightened kitten.</u>

4. Proofread Ellen's sentences. Find four spelling and punctuation mistakes. Write the sentences correctly.

> 1. We need cookies, bread, and a gallon of milk from the market.
> 2. Theives stole, apples, pears, and grapes from our picnic basket.
> 3. Bob, Jim, and I, stayed untill twelve o'clock.

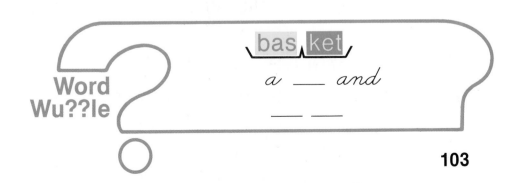

Word Wu??le

⟍bas⟍ket⟋

a ___ and

___ ___

Sound out the words. Then read the story.

concern	elbow	absent	magnet	helmet	until
sixteen	perform	custom	umpire	indeed	pennant
husband	unless	observe	entire	cartoon	cactus

"I do admire your gold links, Nancy," said Peggy Harmon. "Get them fastened together. They'd make a perfect bracelet."

"I can't afford to," said Nancy. "I have only three dollars. I suppose Mr. Barton will charge more."

"Hello, girls," said Mr. Barton as they entered his shop. "What's your problem?"

"I have these four pieces of a gold bracelet," said Nancy, as she laid them on a velvet cloth on his counter. "How much would it cost to attach the pieces?"

"Let's see. I'd have to cut four links and weld them together. The standard price to cut and weld one link is two dollars. But we won't argue. I'll give you a bargain. One dollar each to cut and weld four links," said Mr. Barton.

"Oh, dear!" Nancy said. "That would be four dollars!"

"Correct!" replied Mr. Barton. "I suspect that's as cheap as you'll get."

"Pardon me, Mr. Barton," said Peggy. "I can make the bracelet by cutting and welding only three links."

What do you think Peggy suggested?

Test

23 Rocket Secrets

agree
across
apron
declare
degree
despair
respect
replace
retreat
secret
between
program
ⓢ nothing
chicken
rocket
pocket
jacket
ticket
bucket
ⓢ bushel

In ⌣VCC⌣V⌣ words, the eye-syllables break *after* the CC letters.

rock⌣et⌣
VCC⌣V

In ⌣V⌣CCV⌣ words, the eye-syllables break *before* the CC letters.

se⌣cret⌣
V⌣CCV

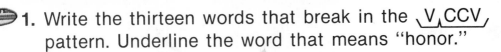

1. Write the thirteen words that break in the ⌣V⌣CCV⌣ pattern. Underline the word that means "honor."

2. Write the words that break in the $\underset{\smile}{VCC}\underset{\smile}{V}$ pattern.

3. Write the picture words. Underline /prō′ gram/.

 **a.**

 b.

 **c.**

 d.

 **e.**

 **f.**

Working with the Words

Dictionary Skills

Sometimes a dictionary gives a phrase /frāz/, or sentence part, to show meanings.

retreat /rē trēt′/ *v.* Go back; withdraw. —*n.* The act of going back or withdrawing: *the retreat of the army.*

1. Write **secret, agree,** and **declare**. Underline the word the Spelling Dictionary uses in a phrase.

2. Write a phrase to show the meanings of these nouns.

    a. bushel (n.)   **b.** respect (n.)

3. Write a phrase to show the meanings of these verbs.

   a. replace (v.)   **b.** respect (v.)

> **An adjective** is a describing word.
> An **adverb** is a word that tells **where, how, how much,** etc.

4. Write the sentences. Draw one line under each adjective and two lines under each adverb.

   a. What is the distance across?

   b. She is using a secret code.

Spelling Helps Language

1. Use words from the Spelling Helps Reading list on page 109 to write synonyms for these words.

   a. sly   **b.** collect

a gree
a cross
a pron
de clare
de gree
de spair
re spect
re place
re treat
se cret
be tween
pro gram
no thing
chick en
rock et
pock et
jack et
tick et
buck et
bush el

Word Wu??le

YOU SECRET ME

a __ __

__ *and* __

The abbreviation for **bushel** and **bushels** is **bu.**
We use **bu.** on tags, signs, etc.
We use **bushel** in sentences like this:

There are four pecks in one **bushel.**

2. Write this sentence. Use the Spelling Dictionary to find the correct numeral to use in the space.

There are ___ quarts in one bushel.

3. Write the VCCV antonyms.

   a. clean   **b.** brave

   c. proud   **d.** everything

   e. awake   **f.** scatter

4. Proofread the letter. Write it correctly.

Dear Mr. Foster
    Please except this ticket
for the thanksgiving Day
program. We're all looking
forwerd to seeing you there
            Yours truly,
            Patrick Finn

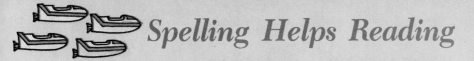

Spelling Helps Reading

library	gather	checkers	reflect	cricket
ashamed	reckon	dirty	whether	asleep
awhile	tricky	afraid	afloat	ashore

"Well, Ethan," said Richard Macklin, "those are the problems we had at school while you were absent. And here are the library books I got you this morning."

"I declare, Richard," said Ethan's mother, "you're a kind person to spend your Saturday mornings helping Ethan. I reckon you'd rather play hockey. I hear you're their best player. I'm afraid Ethan will be out two more weeks."

Richard stuck his hands in his jacket pocket. He did regret missing the games. But Ethan was his friend.

"I'm glad to help, ma'am," he said. "I'll be back without fail next Saturday. I give you my word."

But the next Saturday, just as Richard was starting across the street, his teammates came by.

"Come on, Rich," they cried. "We're playing the Rockets this morning. We need you. It's no secret that we can't win this last big contest without you. Come on!"

What did Richard do?

How many VCCV words are in the story?

 *Test*

polite ✓
tiger ✓
below
begin
direct ✓
protect
behave
thousand
bacon
depend
equal
pupil
poison ✓
report ✓
reward ✓
recess
adult
amount
among
remove

24 Polite Tiger Words

The words in the spelling list are two-syllable words with the **V**owel-**C**onsonant-**V**owel letter pattern.

Break the words into eye-syllables before the consonant letter. Spell each eye-syllable as you spell an accented one-syllable word. But always say the whole word by ear-syllables.

1. Write the words that start with /p/.
Underline /poiʹ sən/.

2. Write the words that start with /b/.
Underline /bā′ kən/.

3. Write the words that start with these sounds.
Circle the word that means "one hundred tens."

/th/	/t/	/ē/
/d/	/d/	/r/
/r/	/r/	/r/

4. Write **among, adult,** and **amount.** Underline
the snurk.

Working with the Words

Dictionary Skills

A dictionary shows all of the correct
pronunciations of entry words.

adult /ə dult′/ *or* /ad′ ult/ *adj.*
Full-grown. —*n.* A full-grown
person or animal.

1. Write **recess, reward,** and **report** in the order they
come in the Spelling Dictionary. Underline the
words for which two pronunciations are given.

2. Write **polite, protect, pupil,** and **poison** in
alphabetical order. Write **n.** after the words that
may be used as **nouns.** Write **adj.** after the word
that may be used as an **adjective.**

3. Write the eye-syllables of each word. As you write an eye-syllable, say and spell it like a one-syllable word. Say the whole word by ear-syllables.

	Eye-Syllables	Ear-Syllables
a. tiger	_____/ _____/	/tī′ gər/
b. thousand	_____/ _____/	/thou′ zənd/
c. adult	_____/ _____/	/ə dult′/
d. equal	_____/ _____/	/ē′ kwəl/
e. among	_____/ _____/	/ə mung′/
f. bacon	_____/ _____/	/bā′ kən/

Spelling Helps Language

Three abbreviations can be used for **quart:** **qt., qu.,** or **q.** The one we use most often is **qt.** The abbreviation for **quarts** can be **qt.** or **qts.** The abbreviation for **pint** is only **pt.** For **pints** it is only **pts.**

1. Write **4 qts. = 1 gal.** and **1 pt. = ½ qt.** as sentences without abbreviations. Spell out the number words.

2. Use words from the spelling list and from the Spelling Helps Reading list to write VCV synonyms for these words.

   a. outcome   **b.** start

   c. account   **d.** grown-up

   e. straight   **f.** sum

3. Use words from the lists to write VCV antonyms.

   a. end   **b.** smart

   c. above   **d.** given

   e. child   **f.** teacher

4. Proofread the sentences and write them correctly. Write **True** or **False** after each sentence.

1. A pupil may be either an addult or a child.
2. A thousand pennies equals ten dollers.
3. A tiger is yellow with black spots.
4. The word's protect and respect have the same meaning.
5. Recess is the time too play.

po lite

ti ger

be low

be gin

di rect

pro tect

be have

thou sand

ba con

de pend

e qual

pu pil

poi son

re port

re ward

re cess

a dult

a mount

a mong

re move

113

Spelling Helps Reading

spider	event	along	pony	omit	stupid
alert	result	raisin	tulip	acorn	taken
spoken	delight	hero	around	motel	stolen

The moment Susan Davis stepped into Hobart's store to select a gift, she heard the tinkle of glass. Elaine Graham, her classmate, was alone at the counter. Susan saw Elaine replace a tiny flower vase on its base so it would not seem broken. Susan pretended she had not noticed.

Elaine had many friends among the pupils at school, and Susan wanted to be her friend, too.

"Hi, Susan," said Elaine politely. "I can't seem to find what I want here. I'll see you around."

Elaine smiled as she slipped out the door. Susan saw that Mr. Hobart was busy showing something to Homer Gleason. That pest, Homer! Nobody liked him. Susan didn't because he teased her and made fun of her at school.

As Homer and Mr. Hobart returned, Homer's shoulder brushed along the counter. Crash! The tiny vase fell to the floor in two parts. Mr. Hobart's face got red.

"The label on that vase shows that it costs five dollars!" shouted Mr. Hobart. "You're going to pay for it!"

What would you do if you were Susan?

Test

114

25 Rapid Travel Words

forest
divide
planet
cabin
comet
disease
robin
lemon
closet
spinach
shadow
loosen
vanish
limit
rapid
widow
radish
parent
salad
dozen

The words in the list are two-syllable words with the **Vowel-Consonant-Vowel** pattern. Break the words into eye-syllables after the consonant letter.

rap᠎id
VC↑V

trav᠎el
VC↑V

Spell each eye-syllable as you spell an accented one-syllable word. Say the whole word by ear-syllables.

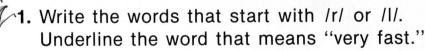

1. Write the words that start with /r/ or /l/. Underline the word that means "very fast."

115

for‿est‿
div‿ide‿
plan‿et‿
cab‿in‿
com‿et‿
dis‿ease‿
rob‿in‿
lem‿on‿
clos‿et‿
spin‿ach‿
shad‿ow‿
loos‿en‿
van‿ish‿
lim‿it‿
rap‿id‿
wid‿ow‿
rad‿ish‿
par‿ent‿
sal‿ad‿
doz‿en‿

2. Write the words that start with /d/ or /k/. Circle the snurk.

3. Write the picture words. Underline /sal′ əd/.

a.   **b.**   **c.**

4. Write the words for these meanings.

    a. go away   **b.** mother or father   **c.** illness

5. Write **widow, spinach,** and **shadow.**
Underline the word with /ch/.

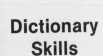

Working with the Words

Dictionary Skills

Any vowel letter can spell the /ə/ sound.

salad /sal′ <u>ə</u>d/   **loosen** /lü′ s<u>ə</u>n/

robin /rob′ <u>ə</u>n/   **lemon** /lem′ <u>ə</u>n/

circus /sėr′ k<u>ə</u>s/

1. Write **loosen, salad, lemon, robin,** and **circus.**

    Underline the letters that spell the /ə/ sound.

2. Fit the eye-syllables together to spell VCV words.

First eye·syllable: cab spin clos loos shad
Second eye·syllable: ach in et ow en

Spelling Helps Language

The abbreviation **doz.** stands for **dozen,** one or more groups of twelve. We use **dozens,** and not the abbreviation, in sentences like this:

Dozens of birds flocked to the bird feeder.

1. Write a few sentences about a widow who divided two dozen cookies among children who shoveled snow for her. Use an abbreviation.

2. Proofread the word lists. Write the misspelled words correctly.

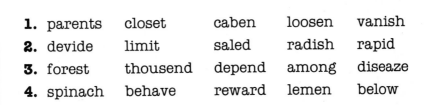

1.	parents	closet	caben	loosen	vanish
2.	devide	limit	saled	radish	rapid
3.	forest	thousend	depend	among	diseaze
4.	spinach	behave	reward	lemen	below

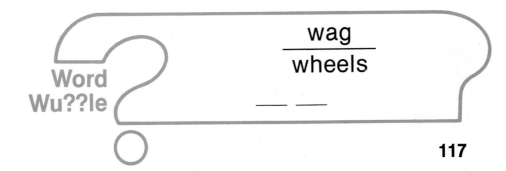

Word Wu??le

wag
wheels

___ ___

117

Spelling Helps Reading

Sound out the words.

decade	shrivel	tepid	mimic	prison	pedal
olive	wizard	petal	punish	seven	exit
chisel	timid	travel	panic	tenant	wagon

Choose the meanings of the underlined words.

1. The <u>decade</u> from 1950 to 1960 was a lively time.

      a. a long time   **b.** ten years   **c.** one year

2. "A stitch in time saves nine" is an old <u>maxim</u>.

      a. sentence   **b.** noun   **c.** rule

3. Rabbits are shy and <u>timid</u> and do not fight their foes.

      a. easy to frighten   **b.** small   **c.** bold

4. The fire in the building caused a <u>panic</u>.

      a. noise   **b.** long absence   **c.** great fear

5. Building owners like neat <u>tenants</u>.

      a. good friends   **b.** rent payers   **c.** painters

6. When we have no rain, our plants <u>shrivel</u> and die.

      a. come out   **b.** bud   **c.** dry up

7. The water stood in the sun and became <u>tepid</u>.

      a. dirty   **b.** boiling   **c.** warm

8. Our parrot can <u>mimic</u> our voices.

      a. scream   **b.** copy   **c.** sing

Test

26 Modern Music Words

Some VCV words break into eye-syllables after the consonant.

\mod‚ern⁄
VC↑V

Some VCV words break into eye-syllables before the consonant.

\mu‚sic⁄
V↑CV

Spell VCV eye-syllables as you spell one-syllable words. Say the whole word by ear-syllables.

1. Say the spelling words.
Listen for the loud syllables.
Write words with the loud second syllable.

famous
season
repeat
salute
demand
provide
minus
aloud
hotel
human
moment
pilot
habit
polish
modern
heavy
busy
desert
desert
lever
lever
record
record

2. Write the eight ‿VC‿V‿ words. Circle the snurks.

3. Write the fifteen ‿V‿CV‿ words. Underline the word that means "well known."

Working with the Words

Dictionary Skills

The word ‿**rec‿ord**‿ /rek′ ərd/ is a noun.

The word ‿**re‿cord**‿ /rē kôrd′/ is a verb.

record /rē kôrd′/ *v.* Set down in writing; make a record. /rek′ ərd/ — *n.* Written account.

1. Find **record** in the Spelling Dictionary. Write a sentence using **record** as a noun and another sentence using **record** as a verb.

2. Write the **ed** and **ing** forms of these verbs.

a.

b.

3. Find **desert** and **lever** in the Spelling Dictionary. Write these sentences. Use **noun** or **verb** in each space.

a. The word **desert** /dez′ərt/ is a ___.

b. The word **desert** /də zėrt′/ is a ___.

c. The word **lever** /lev′ ər/ or /lē′ vər/ is a ___.

4. Use words from the spelling list to fill the spaces. Write the sentences. Underline all of the nouns.

a. She kept a good ___ of her trip across the ___.

b. We have very ___ rainfalls at this ___ of the year.

c. Does a ___ pull a ___ to start the plane?

d. Wait a ___, and I'll help you ___ the car.

fa mous
sea son
re peat
sa lute
de mand
pro vide
mi nus
a loud
ho tel
hu man
mo ment
pi lot
hab it
pol ish
mod ern
heav y
bus y
de sert
des ert
le ver
lev er
re cord
rec ord

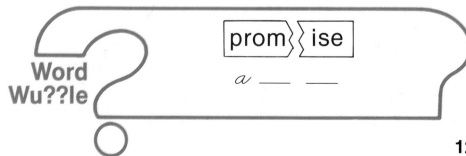

Word Wu??le

prom⟨⟨ ise

a __ __

Spelling Helps Language

The abbreviation for **mile** and **miles** is **mi.**
We use **mi.** on road signs and maps. We do not use **mi.** in a sentence like this:

The hotel is ten **miles** from the airport.

1. Write **mile** and the words from the list on page 123 in which **i**-consonant-**e** spells /ī/ in the loud syllable.

When a speaker's words end with an exclamation mark, we put the quotation marks after the exclamation mark.
  Janet yelled, "Pull the lever!"

2. Proofread the speech balloons. Write what each child is saying. Use **called, replied,** and **said.**

Spelling Helps Reading

Sound out the words.

alone	cement	prepare	nylon	alike	pretend
alive	model	alarm	female	finish	metal
giraffe	promise	honest	risen	satin	visit
panel	humid	student	notice	total	robot

Choose the word in each row that does not belong.
V CV words do not belong with VC V words.

1. bacon   season   amount   cement   (metal)
2. robin   stolen   modern   pedal   tenant
3. motel   widow   radish   punish   satin
4. tulip   spider   timid   pupil   poison
5. acorn   delight   polite   lemon   below
6. tiger   habit   disease   visit   vanish
7. minus   hotel   human   equal   limit
8. pilot   planet   moment   total   behave

Desert /də zėrt'/ and **dessert** are homonyms.
To **desert** means "to leave a person or thing
that should not be left." A **dessert** is a
treat after a meal.

Test

123

giant
trial
diet
science
fuel
lion
ruin
liar
real
cruel
dial
poem
quiet
radio
diamond
museum
violin
idea
 piano
piano
usual

27 Giant Lion Words

Giant Lion words have the **V**owel-**V**owel pattern.
The two vowel letters spell two vowel sounds.
Break **VV** words into eye-syllables <u>between</u> the vowels.

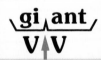

Spell each eye-syllable as a one-syllable word.

Say the whole word by ear-syllables.

1. Write the six words with **ia** together.
   Circle the snurk.

2. Write the six words with **ie** or **io** together.
Underline the three-syllable words.

3. Write **fuel, cruel, ruin,** and **usual.**
Put a check over each vowel letter.

rŭĭn

4. Write **poem, museum, real,** and **idea.**
Put a check over each vowel letter.

ĭdĕă

Working with the Words

Dictionary Skills

/zh/ shows the sound that ends .

Hear /zh/ in **usual.** **/ū′ zhü əl/**

1. Write the words with these pronunciations.

a. /mū zē′ əm/   **b.** /ī dē′ ə/   **c.** /kwī′ ət/

d. /pē an′ ō/   **e.** /ū′ zhü əl/   **f.** /sī′ əns/

2. Write the picture words.

a.

b.

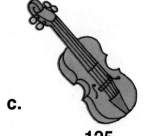

c.

125

3. Write the sentences using words from the spelling list.

    a. The **c** is silent after **s** in **scene** and ___.

    b. The **qu** spells /kw/ in **quarter** and ___.

    c. The **o** spells the /ə/ sound in **lemon**, ___, and ___.

    d. The **u** spells the /ə/ sound in **circus** and ___.

Spelling Helps Language

The abbreviation for **inch** and **inches** is **in.**

A symbol for **inch** or **inches** is **"** .
The abbreviation for **foot** and **feet** is **ft.**

A symbol for **foot** or **feet** is **'** .
A board that is one **foot** and 7 **inches** long and 6 **inches** wide could be labeled in these two ways:

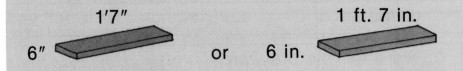

    1'7"   1 ft. 7 in.

6"   or   6 in.

1. Write a sentence in which you compare the lengths of a **radio** which is 12" long and a **violin** which is 2' long. Use two abbreviations.

2. Write the VV words. Use the spelling
list and Spelling Helps Reading list.

   a. You can fiddle with it.

   b. You would find it on a desert.

   c. It is where an artist works.

   d. You burn it to make heat and light.

   e. It is a place to sit outdoors.

> We use commas in sentences to tell the
> reader to pause and then go on.
>
> As you know, the **c** is silent in **science.**
>
> Yes, a diamond is a gem stone.

3. Proofread the sentences and write them
correctly.

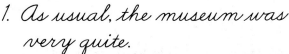

   1. As usual, the museum was
     very quite.
   2. No the giant in this old tail
     was not at all cruel.
   3. "Tell me your secret," she demanded.
   4. Are the flowers on the piano reel.

gi ant
tri al
di et
sci ence
fu el
li on
ru in
li ar
re al
cru el
di al
po em
qui et
ra di o
di a mond
mu se um
vi o lin
i de a
pi an o
u su al

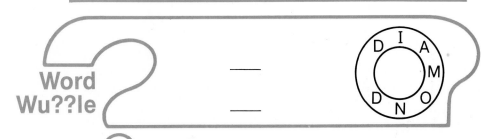

Word Wu??le

D I A
M
D O
N

___
___

127

Spelling Helps Reading

Sound out the words.

pioneer	area	patriot	stadium	duel	duet
patio	oasis	medium	theater	riot	gradual
rodeo	poet	studio	diary	violet	genius

Complete the sentences.

1. **Giant** is to **dwarf** as **lion** is to . . .
   - **a.** tiger
   - **b.** giraffe
   - **c.** (mouse)

2. **Dial** is to **radio** as **key** is to . . .
   - **a.** metal
   - **b.** lock
   - **c.** carton

3. **Quiet** is to **noisy** as **cruel** is to . . .
   - **a.** gentle
   - **b.** real
   - **c.** tough

4. **Oasis** is to **traveler** as **cabin** is to . . .
   - **a.** area
   - **b.** pioneer
   - **c.** castle

5. **Fuel** is to **fire** as **food** is to . . .
   - **a.** diet
   - **b.** farmer
   - **c.** saucer

6. **Medium** is to **superior** as **usual** is to . . .
   - **a.** fair
   - **b.** poor
   - **c.** ideal

Pliers? Liars?
Diary? Dairy?
Flyers? Choirs?
Cruel? Very!

Test

128

28 Pirate Captains

advice
notice
office
practice
justice
ˢ police
remain
contain
mountain
fountain
certain
captain
relate
private
pirate
enchant
vacant
instant
merchant
ˢ pleasant

Loud syllables are easy to spell because you can hear their vowel sounds.

Soft syllables are hard to spell because their vowel sounds are not clear.

ad vice
re main

no tice
moun tain

Say the soft syllables to yourself as if they were loud syllables. Then spell them as if they really were loud syllables.

 1. Write the six **ice** words. Circle the snurk.

ad vice
no tice
of fice
prac tice
jus tice
po lice
re main
con tain
moun tain
foun tain
cer tain
cap tain
re late
pri vate
pi rate
en chant
va cant
in stant
mer chant
pleas ant

2. Write the **ain** words. Circle the word for "sure."

3. Write the **ate** words. Circle the word that means "not for the public."

4. Write the **ant** words. Circle the snurk.

Working with the Words

Dictionary Skills

Practice, the verb, can be spelled **practise. Practice,** the noun, is always spelled **practice. practice** /prak′ təs/ *n.* Action repeated to gain skill. —*v.* Repeat something to learn it. **practiced, practicing.** Also, **practise.**

1. Write **practice** and the other words that end with /əs/.

2. Write ⛰ and the other words that end with /tən/.

3. Write 🏴‍☠️ and the other word that ends with /ət/.

130

Spelling Helps Language

The abbreviation for **mountain** and **mount** is **mt.** We start this abbreviation with capital **M** when it is used in place names like **Mt. Hood** and **Mt. Rushmore.**

1. Write one sentence with the word **mountain** and one sentence with the abbreviation **Mt.**

2. Write sentences about a pirate who notices a half-buried chest and finds that it contains diamond jewels.

3. **Proper nouns** like **Alice, Captain Bly,** and **Fountain St.** start with capital letters. **Proofread** these sentences. Find a "proper noun" mistake and another mistake. Write the sentences correctly.

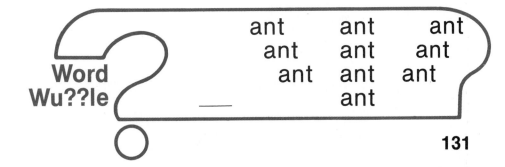

Mt. McKinley is located in alaska. It is the highest mountain peek in all of North America.

Word Wu??le

	ant	ant	ant
	ant	ant	ant
	ant	ant	ant
	___	ant	

131

Spelling Helps Reading

Sound out the words.

device	complain	climate	gallant	hydrant
service	obtain	debate	tyrant	servant
curtain	senate	dictate	constant	tenant

Choose the correct meanings of the underlined words.

1. Alice lost her dime in a <u>crevice</u> in the sidewalk.
    a. pothole   **b.** cement   **c.** crack

2. We need some kind of <u>device</u> to cut metal.
    a. plan   **b.** slicer   **c.** tool

3. The <u>constant</u> ticking of the clock droned on for hours.
    a. loved   **b.** pleasant   **c.** never stopping

4. The <u>fragrant</u> odor of the roses was pleasant.
    a. sweet-smelling **b.** full-grown **c.** bitter

5. The <u>tenants</u> in the new building paid high rents.
    a. renters   **b.** owners   **c.** workers

6. The cruel <u>tyrant</u> made slaves of his people.
    a. queen   **b.** prince   **c.** unjust ruler

Soft-syllable vowels are hard to hear,
So <u>think</u> them loud and make them clear.

Test

132

Soft syllables are hard to spell because their vowel sounds are not clear.

pic ture   mes sage

Say the soft syllables to yourself as if they were loud syllables. Then spell them as if they were loud syllables.

1. Write the **age** snurks. Underline the /zh/ word.

2. Write the seven **age** words that are not snurks.

message
manage
cottage
package
bandage
garbage
damage
garage
courage
language
picture
pasture
creature
capture
future
mixture
nature
treasure
measure
pleasure

133

mes,sage,
man,age,
cot,tage,
pack,age,
ban,dage,
gar,bage,
dam,age,
ga,rage,
cour,age,
lan,guage,
pic,ture,
pas,ture,
crea,ture,
cap,ture,
fu,ture,
mix,ture,
na,ture,
trea,sure,
mea,sure,
plea,sure,

3. Write the seven **ture** words. Circle the word that means "grazing land."

4. Write the **sure** snurks. Underline each **s** that spells /zh/.

Working with the Words

1. Write the /chər/ words. Underline .

2. Write the /zh/ words. Underline .

3. Write the /ij/ words. Underline .

4. Write the correct words. Spell them right.

a. /gə räzh′/
or
/gär′ bij/

b. /man′ ij/
or
/mes′ ij/

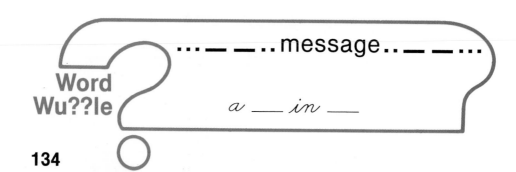

Word Wu??le

…▬ ▬..message..▬ ▬…

a ___ in ___

134

Spelling Helps Language

Capt. is the abbreviation for **Captain.** The abbreviation is used only with a person's name.

Capt. Smith is proud of his ship.
He is a fine **captain.**

1. Write sentences about a pirate, Capt. Kidd, and buried treasure. Try to use **pleasure, capture, manage, message,** and **courage.**

2. Write synonyms from the spelling list for these words.

   a. harm   **b.** note   **c.** joy

3. **Proofread** the lists of noun and adjective snurks. Two are in the wrong list. One is misspelled. Write the lists correctly.

Nouns	Adjectives
1. pleasure	1. busy
2. pleasant	2. heavy
3. treasure	3. salad
4. language	4. usual
5. courage	5. fierse

Sound out the words.

storage	village	cabbage	passage	fixture
moisture	image	puncture	fracture	baggage
savage	luggage	venture	vulture	pasture
feature	torture	sausage	postage	lecture

Unscramble the ten sentences and mark them **True** or **False**.

1. storage can be in furniture put
2. can a storms cottage damage
3. some creatures produces nature strange
4. courage to put a person on a bandage needs
5. a good garage is in garbage to store
6. to find a rich pleasure it's a treasure
7. to manage a clever message can send a spy home
8. of their artists pictures may paints in a use mixture
9. adventures sailors often have on their voyages
10. creature a vulture tiny a is

In words like **guard** and **guess** the **u** after **g** signals that **g** really spells /g/ and not /j/. Sometimes **gu** spells /gw/ as in **language.**

Test

136

30 Beauty Snurks

The words in the spelling list are **two-syllable snurks** with unexpected spellings.

sol = /sōl/ **dier** = /jər/

sol dier

To spell snurks, we find the unexpected spellings — and remember them.

 1. Write the correct snurks.

    a. ea spells /ē/ in **eat** and **season,** but not in these four snurks.

137

enough
country
cousin
stomach
echo
machine
jealous
weather
minute
obey
toward
iron
ocean
against
woman
women
believe
oven
~~beauty~~
soldier

e̦nough

coun̦try

coușin

stom̦ach

ech̦o

ma̦chine

jeal̦ous

weath̦er

min̦ute

o̦bey

to̦ward

i̦ron

o̦cean

a̦gainst

wo̦man

wo̦men

be̦lieve

ov̦en

beau̦ty

sol̦dier

b. ou spells /ou/ in **out** and **about,** but not in these four snurks.

c. ch spells /ch/ in **chop** and **rich,** but not in these three snurks.

2. An **o** followed by a consonant letter spells /o/ in **cot** and **copper,** but not in the loud syllables of these five snurks.

3. Write the snurks with these unexpected spellings.

a. **ie** spells /ē/

b. **ai** spells /e/

c. **oward** spells /ôrd/

d. **bey** spells /bā/

e. **ute** spells /ət/

f. **ron** spells /ərn/

g. **eau** spells /ū/

h. **dier** spells /jər/

i. **gh** spells /f/

j. **ov** spells /uv/

4. Use these snurks and review words to form a sentence. Remember the period.

ocean   swim   The   warm   weather

the   enough   to   in   is

138

Working with the Words

Dictionary Skills

Some dictionaries show three ways to pronounce **toward**.

/tôrd/ or /tōrd/ or /tə wôrd'/

1. Write **toward, against,** and **minute.** Circle the word for which the dictionary gives two pronunciations.

2. Write the plurals of **woman, country,** and **machine.**

3. Write the picture words.

a. **b.** **c.**

Spelling Helps Language

The abbreviation for **yard** is **yd.** The abbreviation for **yards** is **yd.** or **yds.**

One **yard** of cloth would have been enough. The length of the leather belt was 2 **yds.** 3 ft. = 1 **yd.**

1. There are eight different snurks in the sample sentences in the abbreviation story. Write the snurks.

2. Use Spelling Helps Reading words to write antonyms.

    a. least   **b.** better

    c. old   **d.** falsehood

    e. hate   **f.** back

3. Use words from both lists to write the synonyms.

    a. hunt   **b.** plenty   **c.** sea

4. Proofread the list of adjectives. Find two misspelled words and two words that are not used as adjectives. Write the list correctly.

> 1. vacant   5. obey
> 2. certian   6. bisy
> 3. jealous   7. pleasant
> 4. pretty   8. pause

5. Use adjectives from Exercise 4 for the pictures.

    a.    **b.**    **c.**

Word Wu??le

〈up〉 it

___ ___ ___

140

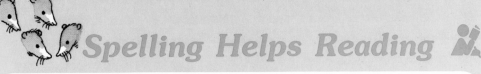

Spelling Helps Reading

Read the snurks and the verse.

does	water	course	search	truth	heart
said	want	they	shoe	worse	shove
where	laugh	both	love	shall	great
of	mother	guess	young	their	though
most	what	bear	world	break	leather
through	have	was	watch	eye	been
other	here	pretty	friend	touch	front
would	one	any	give	group	word

All: Spelling tests are bad **enough,**
But <u>twenty</u> snurks? I call that **tough.**

Girl 1: Just when I learn to do my duty
They make me spell a word like **beauty!**

Boy 1: I can make out with **gas-o-line,**
But **iron? oven? wash machine?**

Girl 2: I do not mind a word like **board,**
But I don't like the one spelled **toward.**

Boy 2: I hear the sounds I spell in **limit,**
But, **cousin,** take a look at **minute.**

Girl 3: I think I'd like to make a motion
To write about a sea (not **ocean**).

All: Snurks are sneaky, snurks are **rough.**
Twenty snurks? That's quite **enough!**

Test

joyous
nervous
▽dangerous
curious
furious
▽anxious
▽serious
cheerful
grateful
▽beautiful
infant
elegant
silent
different
▽terrible
possible
honorable
probable
careless
▽breathless

31 Joyous Words

An adjective suffix is a word part we add to a word
or word root to change it into an adjective.

Root	**Suffix**	**Adjective**
↓	↓	↓
joy	**+** **ous**	**=** **joyous**

Spell each word part as you spell a little word.

 1. Write the three **ful** adjectives. Circle the snurk.

2. Write the two **less** adjectives. Circle the snurk.

142

3. Write the seven **ous** and **ious** adjectives. Underline each adjective ending.

4. Write the four **ible** and **able** adjectives. Underline each adjective ending.

5. Write the four **ant** and **ent** words. Underline the word that can be used as a noun and as an adjective.

Working with the Words

Dictionary Skills	Dictionaries list some suffixes as entry words. —**ful** *suffix* used to form adjectives. **1.** Full of ___: *Cheerful* means *full of cheer.* **2.** Showing ___: *Careful* means *showing care.*

1. Write the **ful, able, ant, ent,** and **less** suffixes in the order they come in the Spelling Dictionary.

2. Write adjectives from the list for the pictures.

a.

b.

c.

Spelling Helps Language

joyous
nervous
dangerous
curious
furious
anxious
serious
cheerful
grateful
beautiful
infant
elegant
silent
different
terrible
possible
honorable
probable
careless
breathless

A **postscript** is a short message added to a letter. The abbreviation for **postscript** is **P.S.**

1. Write the sentence with all the words spelled correctly. Mark the sentence **True** or **False.**

   a. It's /pos′ ə bəl/ to add a /sir′ ē əs/ postscript to a /chir′ fəl/ letter.

   b. The words /sī′ lənt/ and /el′ ə gənt/ have /dif′ ə rənt/ meanings.

   c. The words /grāt′ fəl/ and /thank′ fəl/ are antonyms.

2. **Proofread** these synonym-antonym word pairs to find a spelling mistake and a synonym-antonym mistake. Write the list correctly.

1. lovely – beatiful —— syn.
2. useful – useless ——ant.
3. angry – furious ——ant.

Word Wu??le

ANSWERS
answers

____ ____

144

Sound out the words. Then read the story.

thankful	various	helpless	hopeless	fragrant
absent	painful	visible	peaceable	glorious
fearless	sensible	suitable	gallant	horrible
cautious	agreeable	lawful	hopeful	diligent

Once upon a time the beautiful queen of a distant land called her wise men to her.

"Needless to say, I am grateful for your boundless wisdom, my honorable friends," she said with a cheerful smile. "Your excellent advice has helped me perform my various duties. But I am curious. Who is the most sensible among all of you famous men? I want to find out.

"I have here a scale and six coins. Five coins are gold. They weigh the same. One coin is not true gold. It weighs less than the others. You can't tell which is different by lifting them. You will need to use the scale."

The anxious men present were nervous and silent.

"You can weigh one coin against the others," said the queen. "But then you'd use the scale three times. I am hopeful that you will find it possible to use the scale only twice. Can you do it?"

Suddenly a serious old fellow broke the silence.

"I can!" he cried. "You should...."

Test

145

32 Happiness Words

A noun suffix is a word part we add to a word or word root to change it into a noun.

Root	Suffix	Noun
↓	↓	↓
happy	**+** **ness**	**=** **happiness**

Spell each word part as you spell a little word.

 1. Write the **ment** and **ness** nouns. Circle the snurk.

2. Write the **ance** and **ence** nouns. Circle the snurk.

3. Write the five **ant** and **ent** nouns.

4. Write the five **able** and **tion** nouns. Underline each noun ending.

5. Write the words with these spellings.

   a. ph = /f/   **b. bus** = /biz/   **c. tient** = /shənt/

Working with the Words

Dictionary Skills

In words that come from Greek, we use the letters **ph** to spell /f/.

   tel͵e͵phone͵ /tel′ ə fōn/

   ͵al͵pha͵bet͵ /al′ fə bet/

1. Write **vegetable, elephant,** and **difference.** Underline the word that came into English from Greek.

2. Write the words with these meanings.

   a. word part   **b.** joy   **c.** one who serves

   d. one who studies   **e.** telling sentence   **f.** asking sentence

147

basement

statement

ornament

happiness

business

darkness

vegetable

syllable

student

patient

question

station

nation

servant

hydrant

elephant

attendance

balance

difference

silence

Spelling Helps Language

TV is the abbreviation for **television.**
The abbreviation **TV** is often used as
a word which we pronounce /tē′ vē′/.

1. Write **television, treasure, question,** and **TV**
   in the order they come in the dictionary.

2. In words like **happy,** we change **y** to **i**
   before adding **ness.** Add **ness** to these
   y-ending words to spell new words.

   a. ready   **b.** empty   **c.** silly

3. **Proofread** the sentences and write them
   correctly. Mark each sentence **True** or **False.**

   1. A curious person often
      asks questions.
   2. Thier are four sylables in
      the word *happiness*.
   3. The words *nervious* and *nation*
      are used as nouns.

**Word
Wu??le**

((____books_____books__))

___ *the* ___

Sound out the words. Then read the story.

payment	eagerness	mention	presence	election
talent	entrance	fragrance	accident	stillness
selection	assistant	apartment	likeness	sentence
merchant	action	motion	fraction	direction

Mr. Harkness, a clever salesman, arrived at the bus station. He was ready for some serious business in town.

"Goodness!" he cried, glancing in a mirror. "My hair looks terrible. It would be sensible to get a good haircut before I start selling my goods to these merchants."

Mr. Harkness looked in both directions on Main Street for the location of a suitable barbershop. He saw two.

"Now the question is, which barber is better," he said.

One shop was in the better section of town. Mr. Harkness stared in the window.

"An excellent, prosperous looking shop," he said. "The barber has a marvelous haircut, just the kind I want."

The other was a basement shop that looked as miserable as possible. It would not win any prizes for cleanliness or neatness. The barber was dozing. His hair was long and badly cut. Pausing a moment at the entrance, Mr. Harkness marched in and had his hair cut.

Why did he choose the barber with the bad haircut?

Test

unlike
unload
untie
unfold
unlock
unhappy
unlucky
reappear
recall
restore
repair
remind
rearrange
▽recover
distrust
disappear
disagree
disappoint
dislike
▽discover

33 Discover Words

Prefixes are word parts we add to the front of words or word roots to change their meanings.

Prefix		Root		New Word
↓		↓		↓
un	+	**lock**	=	**unlock**
re	+	**call**	=	**recall**
dis	+	**like**	=	**dislike**

Spell each word part as you spell a little word.

1. The prefix **un** means "not." Write the words with the **un** prefix. Then write them without the prefixes.

2. The prefix **dis** means "the opposite of." Write the words with the **dis** prefix. Then write the same words without **dis.**

3. The prefix **re** means "back" or "again." Write the words with the **re** prefix. Circle the word for "call back."

Working with the Words

Dictionary Skills

Dictionaries show some prefixes as entry words.

re—*prefix* meaning **1.** Again: *Reappear* means *appear again.* **2.** Back: *Recall* means *call back.*

1. Find **dis** in the Spelling Dictionary. Write the three entry words that come just after **dis.**

2. Unscramble the words and write the sentence correctly. Use capital letters and punctuation marks correctly.

I that garage door the unlocked was discovered

unlike
unload
untie
unfold
unlock
unhappy
unlucky
reappear
recall
restore
repair
remind
rearrange
recover
distrust
disappear
disagree
disappoint
dislike
discover

3. Write the words for the pictures correctly.

a. /un hap′ ē/ /stüd′ ənt/   **b.** /un luk′ ē/ /wŭm′ ən/

Spelling Helps Language

The abbreviation for **versus** /vėr′ səs/ is **vs.,** which means "against." Tigers **vs.** Rams means Tigers **against** Rams.

1. Write sentences about losing a ticket to a baseball game. Use **vs., discovered, disappointed,** and **unlucky.**

2. Proofread the word lists. Write them correctly.

1. uneasy	uncertian	rewrit	displease
2. recapsure	disgrace	unkind	disagrea
3. dissappoint	unusual	dismis	disorder

**Word
Wu??le**   re   re   ___

152

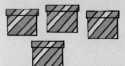

Spelling Helps Reading

Sound out the words. Then read the story.

record	dishonest	unfinished	displace	unfair
uneasy	unkind	disorder	rewrite	unable
uncertain	disgrace	reread	unusual	unfit
unbroken	remark	unknown	displease	unused

"Remember, Janet," remarked Mike, "if you don't win this last game, I remain the unbeaten champ. I regret to tell you that this is the last Ping-Pong ball. We were unable to get any more. Hurry, I must hose the patio."

Mike and Janet were playing Ping-Pong on the patio. To Mike's dismay, Janet refused to quit. She needed two points to unseat him as champ. She smashed the ball past him. He was unable to make a return.

"The ball has disappeared," called Mike. "It rolled down that deep hole. I can see it, but we'll never reach it down there. We'll never recover that ball. This is your unlucky day. You don't win! I'll go get the hose."

Janet peered down the hole in disgust. Then a broad smile returned to her unhappy face.

"I disagree, Mike," she retorted, marching toward the house. "Relax. We'll have that ball back in a few minutes."

How did Janet recover the Ping-Pong ball?

Test

continue
remember
tomato
potato
together
enemy
animal
attention
deliver
banana
bicycle
difficult
telephone
customer
library
electric
already
another
wonderful
handkerchief

34 Electric Words

The words in the spelling list are **three-syllable words.**

Find the eye-syllables. Say each eye-syllable as you would say a one-syllable word. Spell the eye-syllables as you spell one-syllable words.

e lec tric

e | lec | tric

1. Find the three eye-syllables in each word. Say the eye-syllables as if they were three small words.

2. Write the words that have loud <u>second</u> syllables.

3. Write the nine words that have loud <u>first</u> syllables.

4. Write the snurks with these spellings.

    a. ea = /e/   **b. and** = /ang/   **c. on** = /un/

Working with the Words

Dictionary Skills

> **ph** spells /f/ in **alphabet.**
> **alphabet** /al′ fə bet/ *n.* **1.** a, b, c, d, e, etc. **2.** The letters by which we spell sounds.

1. Write the words with /f/.
Underline the letter or letters that spell /f/.

2. Spell the picture words correctly.

    a. /boild/ /pə tā′ tō/   **b.** /rīp/ /tə mā′ tō/

    c. /firs/ /an′ ə məl/   **d.** /hūj/ /bə nan′ ə/

con tin ue
re mem ber
to ma to
po ta to
to geth er
en em y
an im al
at ten tion
de liv er
ba nan a
bi cy cle
dif fi cult
tel e phone
cus tom er
li brar y
e lec tric
al read y
an oth er
won der ful
hand ker chief

Spelling Helps Language

> **Hon.** is the abbreviation for **Honorable,** a title of respect for judges, governors, mayors, etc.

1. Write sentences telling about a mayor's speech on the importance of libraries. Use four spelling words and **Hon.**

2. Proofread the story and write it correctly.

Grandmothers Soap

My grandmother remembers making soap in her own yard. She put grate scoops of lard, grease, and lye together in a huge kettle. The mixture bubbled over a roaring fire. It was poured into a pan to harden. Grandmother says "I made the most wonderful soap in the hole county!"

☛ ✗

Word Wu??le   NME ___

Spelling Helps Reading

Sound out the words. Then read the story.

adventure	entertain	envelope	magazine
satellite	eleven	celebrate	furniture
opposite	separate	neighborhood	decorate
government	hamburger	uniform	mystery

Farmer Jones raised potatoes, tomatoes, and various other crops. On Saturdays his son Jack had to give attention to their farm animals. Mr. Jones would go to town to deliver products to his regular customers.

One Saturday Mr. Jones loaded his truck with several crates of ripe tomatoes. Later, he telephoned Jack to meet him at the hamburger stand for lunch. Jack had ridden to town on his bicycle for some library books. Jack was a whiz at numbers. He was always looking for another book or magazine with number puzzles.

"Well, Dad," said Jack, seating himself opposite his father, "how many crates did you bring in and sell?"

Mr. Jones hesitated a moment. "I sold half of our crates plus a half-crate of tomatoes. I've got one crate left on the truck. Tell me how many crates I started with."

Jack did. Can you?

How many three-syllable words are in the story?

Test

important
regular
history
satisfy
several
hospital
battery
medicine
favorite
separate
president
factory
exercise
probably
grocery
interest
camera
imagine
balcony
company

35 Exercise Words

The words in the list are **three-syllable words.**
Find the eye-syllables. Say the eye-syllables
as you say one-syllable words. Spell the
eye-syllables as you spell one-syllable words.

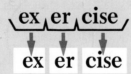

1. Find the three eye-syllables in each word. Say the eye-syllables as if they were three small words.

2. Write the two words with loud second syllables.

158

3. Write the snurks. Circle the word that means "guest."

4. Read the ear-syllables of each word. Write each eye-syllable. Then write the whole word.

a. /sep′ ə rāt/ ⌣sep⌣ ⌣ar⌣ ⌣ate⌣ separate

b. /prez′ ə dənt/ ⌣___⌣ ⌣___⌣ ⌣___⌣ ___

c. /fak′ tə rē/ ⌣___⌣ ⌣___⌣ ⌣___⌣ ___

d. /ek′ sər sīz/ ⌣___⌣ ⌣___⌣ ⌣___⌣ ___

e. /prob′ ə blē/ ⌣___⌣ ⌣___⌣ ⌣___⌣ ___

f. /grō′ sər ē/ ⌣___⌣ ⌣___⌣ ⌣___⌣ ___

g. /med′ ə sən/ ⌣___⌣ ⌣___⌣ ⌣___⌣ ___

h. /kam′ ər ə/ ⌣___⌣ ⌣___⌣ ⌣___⌣ ___

i. /hos′ pi təl/ ⌣___⌣ ⌣___⌣ ⌣___⌣ ___

j. /fā′ vər ət/ ⌣___⌣ ⌣___⌣ ⌣___⌣ ___

⚽⚽ *Working with the Words*

1. Write sentences to show **separate** as a verb and **separate** as an adjective.

2. Write this sentence in regular spelling.
/hē/ /bôt/ /sev′ ər əl/ /kam′ ər ə/ /bat′ ər ēz/

Word Wu??le

— — the ___

President Get

im‚por‚tant
reg‚u‚lar
his‚tor‚y
sat‚is‚fy
sev‚er‚al
hos‚pit‚al
bat‚ter‚y
med‚i‚cine
fa‚vor‚ite
sep‚ar‚ate
pres‚id‚ent
fac‚tor‚y
ex‚er‚cise
prob‚ab‚ly
gro‚cer‚y
in‚ter‚est
cam‚er‚a
im‚a‚gine
bal‚con‚y
com‚pan‚y

3. Write the words with these pronunciations: /his′ tə rē/, /sat′ is fī/, /in′ tər əst/.

Spelling Helps Language

Supt. is the abbreviation for **Superintendent,** a person who manages a factory, school, etc.

Supt. Woods spoke to all new pupils.

1. Write **superintendent**. Write the number of ear-syllables.

2. Proofread this news story. Write it correctly.

> Fourth Grade Visits Airport
>
> Last week Mr. Lanes class spent a day at the airport. Several pupils' thought the control tower was the most interting place they saw their.
>
> Sometimes a pilot cant land at the airport because of bad whether. Then the controllers tell the pilot where to land. A pilots earphones are importent. He uses them to keep in touch with the tower.

160

Spelling Helps Reading

Sound out the words.

detective	consonant	volcano	holiday	memory
realize	contraction	opinion	expensive	committee
recognize	paragraph	alphabet	fortunate	general
telescope	chocolate	astronaut	hesitate	magazine

Choose the word in each row that does not belong.

1. history, science, poetry, grammar, committee

2. umbrella, medicine, bandage, hospital, operation

3. telephone, bicycle, magazine, newspaper, radio

4. satellite, astronaut, volcano, planet, orbit

5. sentence, syllable, language, ornament, alphabet

6. chocolate, strawberry, vanilla, lemon, vegetable

7. general, admiral, soldier, private, captain

8. tomato, turnip, potato, carrot, banana

9. excellent, remarkable, savage, marvelous, beautiful

10. nation, kingdom, republic, village, country

Words like **alphabet,** in which **ph** spells /f/, come from Greek. The first letters of the Greek alphabet are **alpha** and **beta.** We call our ABC's the **alphabet.**

Test

Sunday
▽ *Monday*
Tuesday
▽ *Wednesday*
Thursday
Friday
Saturday
January
February
March
April
May
June
July
August
September
October
November
December

Spell the names of the days and months by breaking each word into eye-syllables. Spell the eye-syllables as you spell one-syllable words.

⎣Ju ⌄ly⎦　　**⎣Sat ⌄ur ⌄day⎦**

Say the whole word by ear-syllables.

⎣Wed ⌄nes ⌄day⎦　　/wenz′ dā/

 1. The names of the days are proper nouns that start with capital letters. Write the names of the days.

2. Names of the months are proper nouns that start with capital letters. Write the names of the months.

3. Write the snurks. Circle the word with three eye-syllables.

Working with the Words

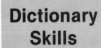

Dictionary Skills

Dictionary symbols show the sounds in **ear-syllables.** Eye-syllables are word parts we see in regular spellings.

1. Write the words for these sound-spellings.

   a. /thėrz′ dā/   **b.** /sat′ ər dā/   **c.** /feb′ rü er′ ē/

   d. /ok tō′ bər/   **e.** /mun′ dā/   **f.** /wenz′ dā/

2. For each symbol below, write a spelling word to show the sound. Use words from any unit.

/a/	cap	/ā/	cake	/ã/	pair		
/e/	get	/ē/	meat	/ä/	barn	/ü/	moon
/i/	big	/ī/	side	/ėr/	her	/ou/	house
/o/	not	/ō/	note	/ô/	lost	/oi/	boy
/u/	mud	/ū/	cute	/u̇/	book	/ə/	circ<u>u</u>s

Sun,day,
Mon,day,
Tues,day,
Wed,nes,day,
Thurs,day,
Fri,day,
Sat,ur,day,
Jan,u,ar,y,
Feb,ru,ar,y,
March
A,pril,
May
June
Ju,ly,
Au,gust,
Sep,tem,ber,
Oc,to,ber,
No,vem,ber,
De,cem,ber,

Spelling Helps Language

Abbreviate the names of days and months like this.

Sun. Mon. Tues. Wed. Thurs. Fri. Sat.

Jan. Feb. Mar. Apr. Aug.

Sept. Oct. Nov. Dec.

1. Write the abbreviation for each word.

   a. Thursday   **b.** November

   c. Monday   **d.** Friday

   e. January   **f.** Wednesday

2. Write a paragraph about your favorite month. Do not use abbreviations unless you are giving a date.

3. Proofread this verse and write it correctly.

Thirty days has september,
April, june, and november.
All the rest have thirty-one,
Save february, which alone
Has twenty-eight and one day more
We add too it one year in fore.

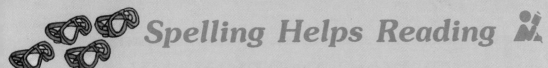

Our Month and Day Names

We get our names for **Sunday, Monday,** and **Saturday** from the Romans. **Sunday** was the "sun" day. **Monday** was their "moon" day. Their god **Saturn** gave his name to **Saturday.**

Tuesday, Wednesday, Thursday, and **Friday** came from the Norse myths. **Tuesday** is from the name of their war god. **Wednesday** is named for the storm god, **Woden.** Thursday **comes from Thor,** the thunder god. **Friday** is named for the Norse goddess of love, **Frigg.**

Our months have Roman names. **January** comes from **Janus,** the god with two faces. **March** is named for **Mars,** the war god. **June** is for **Juno,** queen of the gods. She was also called **Februaria. May** is from **Maia,** another goddess. **April** comes from the Latin word for "open," for the flowers that open in April. **July** was named for **Julius** Caesar, a famous emperor. **August** was named for another emperor, Julius Caesar's nephew, Caesar **Augustus.**

September, October, November, and **December** come from Latin words for "seventh," "eighth," "ninth," and "tenth." **September** was the seventh month because the Roman year began in March.

You've learned to spell? Well, just remember
The words get tougher next September!

Test

SPELLING DICTIONARY

Aa

—able *suffix* used to form adjectives. **1.** Can be ____ ed: *Enjoyable* means *can be enjoyed.* **2.** Suitable for ____: *Comfortable* means *suitable for comfort.*

accept /ak sept′/ *v.* **1.** Take what is offered or given. **2.** Believe. **3.** Say yes to.

account /ə kount′/ *n.* **1.** Explanation. **2.** Statement of money received and spent. —*v.* Consider: *Solomon was accounted wise.*

ache /āk/ *n.* Continuous pain. —*v.* Suffer continuous pain. **ached, aching.**

across /ə krôs′/ *prep.* **1.** Over: *The cat walked across the street.* **2.** Beyond: *The woods are across the river.* —*adv.* From one side to the other: *What is the distance across?*

adj. *abbrev.* for *adjective.*

adjective /aj′ ik tiv/ *n.* Word that describes a person, place, or thing.

admire /ad mīr′/ *v.* Regard with wonder and pleasure. **admired, admiring.**

admit /ad mit′/ *v.* **1.** Say something is real or true. **2.** Allow to enter: *She was admitted to school this year.* **admitted, admitting.**

adult /ə dult′/ *or* /ad′ ult/ *adj.* Full-grown. —*n.* **1.** Grown-up person. **2.** Plant or animal grown to full size or strength.

adv. *abbrev.* for *adverb.*

adverb /ad′ vėrb′/ *n.* Word that tells how, when, where, how much, etc.

advice /ad vīs′/ *n.* Opinion about what should be done.

afford /ə fôrd′/ *v.* Have the money, time, or strength.

against /ə genst′/ *prep.* **1.** In opposition to: *against the law.* **2.** Upon: *The rain beat against the window.* **3.** In preparation for.

agree /ə grē′/ *v.* **1.** Have the same opinion. **2.** Consent. **agreed, agreeing.**

air /ãr/ *n.* **1.** Mixture of gases that surround the earth. **2.** Space overhead. —*v.* Let air through: *air the room.*

airport /ãr′ pôrt′/ *n.* Station with a field for airplanes to land on and take off from.

aloud /ə loud′/ *adj.* Loud enough to be heard; not in a whisper.

already /ôl red′ ē/ *adv.* Before this time; by this time: *You are half an hour late already.*

a.m. *or* **A.M.** The time from midnight to noon.

among /ə mung′/ *prep.* **1.** One of. **2.** In with: *Her brothers were among the crowd.* **3.** Surrounded by: *a house among the trees.* **4.** To each of: *Divide the fruit among the children.*

amount /ə mount′/ *n.* **1.** Total sum: *the amount of the bill.* **2.** Quantity or number of something: *No amount of food would coax the dog from his master.* —*v.* **1.** Reach: *The loss amounts to ten million dollars.* **2.** Be equal: *amounts to stealing.*

—ance *suffix* used to form nouns. **1.** Act or fact of ____ing: *Appearance* means *act or fact of appearing.* **2.** Quality or state of being ____ed: *Annoyance* means *quality or state of being annoyed.* **3.** Quality or state of being ____ant: *Importance* means *state or quality of being important.*

animal /an′ ə məl/ *n.* Any living thing that is not a plant.

ankle /ang′ kəl/ *n.* Joint that connects the foot with the leg.

announce /ə nouns′/ *v.* **1.** Give notice of. **2.** Introduce programs or read news on radio or television. **announced, announcing.**

another /ə nuŦH′ ər/ *adj.* **1.** One more: *Have another glass of milk.* **2.** A different: *Show me another kind of hat.* —*pron.* **1.** One more. **2.** A different one.

answer /an′ sər/ *n.* Words spoken or written in reply to a question. —*v.* **1.** Speak or write in reply to a question. **2.** Act in return to a call or signal: *She answered the doorbell.*

—ant *suffix* used to form adjectives or nouns. *adj.* That ____s or is ____ing: *Pleasant* means *that pleases or is pleasing.* —*n.* One who ____s: *Assistant* means *one who assists.*

ant. *abbrev.* for *antonym.*

antonym /an′ tə nim/ *n.* Word that means the opposite of another: *Up is an antonym of down.*

anxious /angk′ shəs/ *adj.* **1.** Troubled; worried; uneasy. **2.** Wishing very much; eager.

Apr., *abbrev.* for *April.*

April /ā′ prəl/ *n.* The fourth month of the year, following March. April has 30 days.

166

apron /ā′ prən/ *n.* Garment worn over the front part of the body to protect clothes.

aren't /ärnt/ Are not.

argue /är′ gū/ *v.* **1.** Discuss with someone who disagrees. **2.** Give reasons for or against. **argued, arguing.**

arrest /ə rest′/ *v.* **1.** Take to jail or court. **2.** Detain by law. **3.** Stop: *Filling a tooth arrests decay.*

art /ärt/ *n.* **1.** Branch of learning: *History is one of the arts; chemistry is one of the sciences.* **2.** Painting, drawing, and sculpture: *She is studying art.* **3.** Works of art. **4.** Human skill or effort: *the art of self-defense.* **5.** Skillful act: cunning trick: *The fox fooled the hen by its arts.*

attendance /ə ten′ dəns/ *n.* **1.** Attending: *perfect attendance at the meeting.* **2.** Persons attending: *attendance of 200.*

attention /ə ten′ shən/ *n.***1.** Attending: *pay attention.* **2.** Care and thought; consideration: *showed much attention.*

Aug. *abbrev.* for *August.*

August /ô′ gəst/ *n.* The eighth month of the year, following July. August has 31 days.

author /ô′ thər/ *n.* Person who writes books, poems, stories, or articles.

Ave. *abbrev.* for *avenue.*

avenue /av′ ə nū/ *n.* Wide street; road usually bordered by trees.

Bb

bacon /bā′ kən/ *n.* Salted and smoked meat from the back and sides of a pig or hog.

balance /bal′ əns/ *n.* **1.** Instrument for weighing. **2.** Condition of being equal in weight or amount. **3.** A steady position. **4.** Part that is left over; remainder. —*v.* **1.** Put or keep in a steady position. **2.** Weigh two things against one another to see which is heavier. **balanced, balancing.**

balcony /bal′ kə nē/ *n.* **1.** Outside projecting platform with an entrance from an upper floor of a building. **2.** Projecting upper floor in a theater or hall. *pl.* **balconies.**

banana /bə nan′ əl *n.* Slightly curved, yellow fruit with firm, creamy flesh. *pl.* **bananas.**

bandage /ban′ dij/ *n.* Strip of cloth or other material used in binding up a wound. —*v.* Bind with a bandage. **bandaged, bandaging.**

barefoot /bãr′ fût/ *adj.* Without shoes and stockings on: *a barefoot child.*

bargain /bär′ gən/ *n.* **1.** Agreement to trade or exchange. **2.** Something offered or bought cheap. —*v.* Try to make a good deal.

barn /bärn/ *n.* Building for storing hay, grain, etc., and for sheltering farm animals and farm machinery.

basement /bās′ mənt/ *n.* The lowest part of a building, partly or wholly below ground.

bathe /bāŦH/ *v.* **1.** Take a bath. **2.** Give a bath to. **3.** Go swimming. **bathed, bathing.**

bathroom /bath′ rüm′/ *n.* Room fitted out for taking baths.

battery /bat′ ər ē/ *n.* **1.** Single electric cell. **2.** Set of two or more electric cells that produce electric current. **3.** In baseball, the pitcher and catcher together. *pl.* **batteries.**

battle /bat′ əl/ *n.* Fight or contest; warfare. —*v.* Fight; struggle. **battled, battling.**

beat /bēt/ *v.* **1.** Strike again and again. **2.** Overcome; defeat. **3.** Throb: *Her heart beats with joy.* —*n.* **1.** Stroke made again and again; *the beat of the drum.* **2.** Throb: *the beat of his heart.* **3.** Regular round taken by the police or a guard. **4.** Unit of time in music.

beautiful /bū′ tə fəl/ *adj.* Very pleasing to hear or see.

beauty /bū′ tē/ *n.* **1.** Good looks. **2.** Something beautiful. **3.** Quality that pleases in flowers, music, or the like. *pl.* **beauties.**

bedtime /bed′ tīm′/ *n.* Time to go to bed.

beet /bēt/ *n.* Plant grown for its thick, fleshy root. Red beets are eaten as vegetables.

begin /bē gin′/ *v.* **1.** Start. **2.** Come into being: *The club began two years ago.* **began, begun, beginning.**

behave /bē hāv′/ *v.* Act. **behaved, behaving.**

believe /bē lēv′/ *v.* **1.** Think something is true or real. **2.** Have faith; trust. **3.** Think; suppose. **believed, believing.**

below /bē lō′/ *adv.* **1.** In a lower place: *From the plane, we could see the fields below.* **2.** After or later in a book or article: *See the note below.* —*prep.* **1.** Under. **2.** Less than.

bend /bend/ *n.* Part that is not straight; curve; turn: *a bend in the road.* —*v.* **1.** Curve. **2.** Make crooked. **3.** Stoop; bow. **bent, bending.**

/a/ ran   /ā/ rain   /ã/ care   /ä/ car   /e/ hen   /ē/ he   /ėr/ her   /i/ in   /ī/ ice   /o/ not   /ō/ no   /ô/ off   /u/ us
/ū/ use   /ü/ tool   /ů/ took   /ou/ cow   /oi/ boy   /ch/ church   /hw/ when   /ng/ sing   /sh/ ship   /ŦH/ this
/th/ thin   /zh/ vision   /ə/ about, taken, pencil, lemon, circus

between /bē twēn'/ *prep.* **1.** In the time or space separating two objects or places: *There are many cities between Chicago and New York.* **2.** From one to the other of: *a new highway between Chicago and St. Louis.* **3.** Having to do with: *a fight between the two boys.* **4.** In regard to one or the other: *We must choose between the two books.*

bicycle /bī' sik' əl/ *n.* Vehicle with two wheels, one behind the other, which support a metal frame with handles for steering and a seat for a rider. One rides a bicycle by pushing the two pedals with the feet. —*v.* Ride a bicycle. **bicycled, bicycling.**

birthday /bėrth' dā'/ *n.* Day on which a person was born.

blindfold /blīnd' fōld'/ *v.* Cover the eyes of. —*adj.* With eyes covered: *walk blindfold.* —*n.* Thing covering the eyes.

bluebird /blü' bėrd'/ *n.* Small songbird of North America.

bluejay /blü' jā'/ *n.* Noisy, chattering bird with a crest and a blue back.

Blvd. *abbrev.* for *boulevard.*

boathouse /bōt' hous'/ *n.* House or shed where boats are kept.

bold /bōld/ *adj.* **1.** Brave; without fear. **2.** Impudent: *The bold child made faces at us.*

bookcase /bŭk' kās'/ *n.* Piece of furniture with shelves for holding books.

booth /büth/ *n.* **1.** Place where goods are sold or shown. **2.** Small, closed place for telephone. *pl.* **booths** /büths/ *or* /bü<small>TH</small>z/.

bother /bo<small>TH</small>' ər/ *n.* Trouble; much fuss or worry —*v.* **1.** Annoy. **2.** Take trouble: *Don't bother about my breakfast.*

boulevard /bŭl' ə värd/ *n.* A broad street.

bowl[1] /bōl/ *n.* **1.** Hollow, rounded dish. **2.** Amount that a bowl can hold: *a bowl of soup.* **3.** Hollow, rounded part of anything.

bowl[2] /bōl/ *v.* Play the game of bowling.

brave /brāv/ *adj.* Without fear. **braver, bravest.** —*n.* A North American Indian warrior. —*v.* Meet without fear. **braved, braving.**

bread /bred/ *n.* Food made of flour and water or milk and baked.

breath /breth/ *n.* Air drawn into and forced out of the lungs.

breathe /brē<small>TH</small>/ *v.* Draw air into the lungs and force it out. **breathed, breathing.**

breathless /breth' ləs/ *adj.* **1.** Out of breath. **2.** Unable to breathe freely because of fear, interest, or excitement: *The beauty of the scenery left him breathless.*

brow /brou/ *n.* **1.** Forehead. **2.** Eyebrow. **3.** Top or edge: *the brow of a hill.*

bruise /brüz/ *n.* **1.** Injury to the body causing a black-and-blue mark on the skin. **2.** Injury to the outside of a plant. —*v.* Hurt; injure. **bruised, bruising.**

bu. *abbrev.* for *bushel.*

bucket /buk' ət/ *n.* Pail made of wood, metal, or plastic.

bud /bud/ *n.* **1.** Small swelling on a plant that will grow into a flower, leaf, or branch. **2.** Partly opened flower. —*v.* Put forth buds. **budded, budding.**

build /bild/ *v.* **1.** Make by putting materials together. **2.** Develop: *A lawyer must build every case on facts.* —*n.* Form: *the build of an elephant.*

built /bilt/ *v. See* **build.** *The bird built a nest in the tree.*

bulb /bulb/ *n.* **1.** Round, underground bud or stem from which certain plants like onions and tulips grow. **2.** Any object with a rounded end or swelling part: *an electric light bulb.*

burglar /bėr' glər/ *n.* Person who breaks into a building, usually to steal.

bury /ber' ē/ *or* /bėr' ē/ *v.* **1.** Put a dead body in the earth, in a tomb, or in the sea. **2.** Cover up; hide. **buried, burying.**

bushel /bùsh' əl/ *n.* **1.** Measure for grain, vegetables, and other dry things equal to 4 pecks or 32 quarts. **2.** Container that holds a bushel.

business /biz' ə nəs/ *or* /biz' nəs/ *n.* **1.** Work; occupation. **2.** Matter: *This is a serious business.* **3.** Trade; buying and selling: *The store does a big business.* **4.** Store; factory; commercial enterprise: *pl.* **businesses.**

busy /biz' ē/ *adj.* **1.** Having plenty to do. **2.** Full of activity. **3.** In use: *I tried to call him, but his telephone was busy.* **busier, busiest.** —*v.* Make or keep busy. **busied, busying.**

Cc

cabin /kab' ən/ *n.* **1.** Small, roughly built house; hut. **2.** Private room in a ship. **3.** Place for passengers in an aircraft.

camera /kam' ər əl/ *n.* Machine for taking photographs or motion pictures. *pl.* **cameras.**

Capt. *abbrev.* for *captain.*

captain /kap' tən/ *n.* **1.** Head of a group; leader; chief. **2.** Army, airforce, or marine officer ranking below a major. **3.** Navy officer in command of a warship. —*v.* Lead or command.

capture /kap′ chər/ v. **1.** Make a prisoner of. **2.** Catch and keep. **captured, capturing.** —n. Person or thing taken by force.

car /kär/ n. **1.** Automobile. **2.** Any vehicle that moves on wheels. **3.** A railroad car or street-car. **4.** The closed platform of an elevator or airship for carrying people or things.

card /kärd/ n. A flat piece of stiff paper or thin cardboard.

cardboard /kärd′ bôrd′/ n. Stiff material made of layers of paper pressed together, used to make cards and boxes.

carpet /kär′ pət/ n. Heavy woven floor covering. —v. Cover with a carpet.

cartwheel /kärt′ hwēl′/ n. **1.** Wheel of a cart. **2.** Sideways handspring.

castle /kas′ əl/ n. **1.** Large building or group of buildings with thick walls, turrets, battlements, and other defenses against attack. **2.** A piece in a chess game.

cattle /kat′ əl/ n. pl. Cows, bulls, and steers.

cave /kāv/ n. Hollow space underground.

center /sen′ tər/ n. Middle point, place, or part. —v. Collect at the center: *The guests centered around the table.*

certain /sèr′ tən/ adj. **1.** Sure: *It is certain that 2 and 4 do not make 5.* **2.** Some: *Certain plants will not grow here.* **3.** Fixed: *She earns a certain amount of money each week.*

chair /châr/ n. Seat that has a back and, sometimes, arms.

charcoal /chär′ kōl′/ n. Black, brittle form of carbon made by partly burning bones or wood; used as fuel and for drawing.

cheerful /chir′ fəl/ adj. **1.** Glad; full of cheer. **2.** Pleasant; bringing cheer: *a cheerful room.*

chew /chü/ v. Crush or grind with the teeth.

chicken /chik′ ən/ n. Hen or rooster.

chief /chēf/ n. Head of a tribe or group. —adj. Main; most important: *the chief reason.*

child /chīld/ n. **1.** Young boy or girl. **2.** Son or daughter.

choice /chois/ n. Person or thing chosen: *The red hat is my choice.* —adj. Excellent. **choicer, choicest.**

choke /chōk/ v. **1.** Be unable to breathe. **2.** Smother: *choke a fire.* **3.** Control: *choke down your anger.* **4.** Fill up or block: *Sand is choking the river.* **5.** Stop breath by squeezing the throat. **choked, choking.**

choose /chüz/ v. **1.** Pick out; select from a number. **2.** Prefer and decide. **chose, chosen, choosing.**

chore /chôr/ n. Odd job; small task.

chose /chōz/ v. See **choose.** *She chose the red dress.*

cigar /sə gär′/ n. Tight roll of tobacco leaves for smoking.

circle /sèr′ kəl/ n. **1.** A line every point of which is equally distant from the center. **2.** Ring: *We sat in a circle.* **3.** Group of people with the same interests: *a circle of friends.* —v. **1.** Move in a circle. **2.** Surround: *circle the city.* **circled, circling.**

circus /sèr′ kəs/ n. Traveling show of acrobats, clowns, horses, riders, and wild animals. pl. **circuses.**

claim /klām/ v. **1.** Demand as one's own: *Does anyone claim this pencil?* **2.** Say strongly; declare as a fact. —n. **1.** The right to something. **2.** A piece of land which someone claims: *a miner's claim.*

classmate /klas′ māt′/ n. Member of the same class in school.

claw /klô/ n. **1.** Sharp, hooked nail on a bird's or an animal's foot. **2.** Anything like a claw. —v. Scratch, tear, or pull with claws or hands.

clay /klā/ n. A kind of earth that can be shaped when it is wet and hardens when it is dried or baked.

closet /kloz′ ət/ n. Small room used for storing clothes or supplies.

club /klub/ n. **1.** Heavy stick of wood used as a weapon. **2.** Stick used to hit a ball in some games: *golf clubs.* **3.** Group of people joined for some special purpose. —v. Beat or hit with a club. **clubbed, clubbing.**

clue /klü/ n. Fact or object which aids in solving a mystery or problem.

clumsy /klum′ zē/ adj. Awkward in moving. **clumsier, clumsiest.**

clutch /kluch/ v. **1.** Grasp tightly. **2.** Seize. —n. A tight grasp: *The eagle flew off with a rabbit in the clutches of its claws.* pl. **clutches.**

Co. abbrev. for **1.** Company. **2.** County.

coach /kōch/ n. **1.** Carriage. **2.** Passenger car of a railroad train. **3.** Bus. **4.** Person who trains athletic teams. pl. **coaches.** —v. Train or teach: *He coaches the football team.*

coal /kōl/ n. **1.** A black mineral that burns and

/a/ ran /ā/ rain /ä/ care /ă/ car /e/ hen /ē/ he /èr/ her /i/ in /ī/ ice /o/ not /ō/ no /ô/ off /u/ us
/ū/ use /ü/ tool /ů/ took /ou/ cow /oi/ boy /ch/ church /hw/ when /ng/ sing /sh/ ship /ŦH/ this
/th/ thin /zh/ vision /ə/ about, taken, pencil, lemon, circus

gives off heat. **2.** Piece or pieces of this mineral for burning.

coast /kōst/ *n.* Land along the sea. —*v.* Ride or slide without the use of power.

code /kōd/ *n.* **1.** System of secret writing. **2.** System of signals for sending messages. **3.** Set of rules or laws. —*v.* Change into a code: *code a message.* **coded, coding.**

coil /koil/ *v.* Wind around and around into a pile or curl. —*n.* Anything that is coiled: *a coil of rope; a coil of wire.*

collect /kə lekt′/ *v.* **1.** Bring or come together. **2.** Ask and receive pay for debts, dues, etc.

comet /kom′ ət/ *n.* A bright heavenly body with a starlike center and often with a cloudy tail of light. Comets move around the sun in a long oval course.

comfort /kum′ fərt/ *v.* Ease the grief and trouble. —*n.* **1.** Anything that makes grief or trouble easier to bear. **2.** Freedom from hardship: *lives in comfort.*

company /kum′ pə nē/ *n.* **1.** Group of people. **2.** Companions. **3.** Companionship: *My dog is good company.* **4.** Guests; visitors. **5.** Part of an army commanded by a captain. *pl.* **companies.**

conj. *abbrev.* for *conjunction.*

conjunction /kən jungk′ shən/ *n.* A word that connects other words in a sentence. Words like *and, but, while, because* are conjunctions.

contain /kən tān′/ *v.* **1.** Have within itself: *Books contain information.* **2.** Be equal to: *A pound contains 16 ounces.* **3.** Control; hold back: *contain one's anger.*

continue /kən tin′ ū/ *v.* **1.** Keep up; keep on; last: *The rain continued all day.* **2.** Stay: *continue in school.* **continued, continuing.**

cooky /kůk′ ē/ *n.* Small, flat, sweet cake. *pl.* **cookies.** Also spelled **cookie.**

copper /kop′ ər/ *n.* Reddish metal, easy to work with. —*adj.* Made of copper.

copy /kop′ ē/ *n.* **1.** Thing made to be just like another. **2.** One of a number of books, magazines, newspapers, or pictures made at the same printing: *a copy of today's newspaper.* *pl.* **copies** —*v.* **1.** Make a copy of. **2.** Imitate; follow as an example. **copied, copying.**

core /kôr/ *n.* The hard central part containing the seeds of fruits like apples and pears. —*v.* Take out the core of. **cored, coring.**

correct /kə rekt′/ *adj.* **1.** True; right. **2.** Proper. —*v.* Change to what is right.

cottage /kot′ ij/ *n.* **1.** Small house. **2.** House at a summer resort.

country /kun′ trē/ *n.* **1.** Land; region. **2.** All the land of a nation. **3.** People of a nation. **4.** Land outside of cities and towns. *pl.* **countries.** —*adj.* Of the country: *country air.*

county /koun′ tē/ *n.* A district into which a state or country is divided for purposes of government. *pl.* **counties.**

couple /kup′ əl/ *n.* **1.** Two things of the same kind that go together; pair. **2.** Man and woman who are married. —*v.* Join together. **coupled, coupling.**

courage /ker′ ij/ *n.* Bravery; meeting danger without fear.

court /kôrt/ *n.* **1.** Space enclosed by walls or buildings. **2.** Short street. **3.** Place marked off for a game: *a tennis court.* **4.** Followers of a king or queen. **5.** Persons who administer justice; judge or judges. —*v.* **1.** Try to please. **2.** Woo; pay attention in order to marry.

cousin /kuz′ ən/ *n.* Son or daughter of one's uncle or aunt.

cowboy /kou′ boi′/ *n.* Man whose work is looking after cattle on a ranch.

cozy /kō′ zē/ *adj.* Warm and comfortable; snug: *The cat lay in a cozy corner near the fireplace.* **cozier, coziest.**

crazy /krā′ zē/ *adj.* **1.** Having a diseased or injured mind. **2.** Foolish. **3.** Very enthusiastic: *She is so crazy about cats that she brings home every stray she finds.* **crazier, craziest.**

cream /krēm/ *n.* **1.** Part of milk with much butter fat. **2.** Sweet dessert or candy made of cream. **3.** Oily preparation put on skin to make it smooth. —*v.* Make a smooth mixture like cream. —*adj.* Yellowish white.

creature /krē′ chər/ *n.* **1.** Any living person or animal. **2.** Anything created: *Ghosts are creatures of the imagination.*

crew /krü/ *n.* **1.** Men and women doing the work on a ship, aircraft, or the like. **2.** Any group of persons working together.

crook /krůk/ *n.* **1.** Bent or curved part: *the crook of an elbow; a crook in the stream.* **2.** Dishonest person. **3.** Shepherd's staff. —*v.* Bend; make a curve in.

crop /krop/ *n.* Plants grown for their use. —*v.* Cut or bite off the top of: *Sheep had cropped the grass very short.* **cropped, cropping.**

crossroads /krôs′ rōdz′/ *n.* **1.** Roads that cross. **2.** Place where two or more roads cross.

crow[1] /krō/ *n.* Loud cry of a rooster. —*v.* Make the cry. **crowed** or **crew, crowing.**

crow[2] /krō/ *n.* A large, glossy, black bird with a harsh cry.

cruel /krü′ əl/ *adj.* Ready to give pain to others; hard-hearted.

cub /kub/ *n.* Young bear, fox, or lion.

cube /kūb/ *n.* **1.** A solid with 6 square sides, all equal. **2.** Anything shaped like a cube: *ice cube, sugar cube.* —*v.* Make into the shape of a cube. **cubed, cubing.**

cure /kūr/ *n.* Remedy; something that removes or relieves a bad condition or a disease. —*v.* **1.** Make well. **2.** Get rid of. **3.** Preserve meat by drying. **cured, curing.**

curious /kūr′ ē əs/ *adj.* **1.** Eager to know. **2.** Strange; odd; unusual.

curve /kėrv/ *n.* **1.** Line that has no straight part. **2.** Bend in the road. —*v.* Bend so as to form a line that has no straight part. **curved, curving.**

customer /kus′ təm ər/ *n.* Person who buys, especially a regular shopper at a store.

cute /kūt/ *adj.* **1.** Pretty and dear: *a cute baby.* **2.** Clever; cunning: *a cute trick.* **cuter, cutest.**

Dd

damage /dam′ ij/ *n.* Harm or injury that lessens value or usefulness: *the damage to my car.* —*v.* Harm or injure so as to lessen value or usefulness: *I damaged my sweater playing football.* **damaged, damaging.**

danger /dān′ jər/ *n.* **1.** Chance of harm; risk: *A soldier's life is full of danger.* **2.** Thing that may cause harm: *Hidden rocks are a danger to ships.*

dangerous /dān′ jər əs/ *adj.* Likely to cause harm; not safe; risky.

darkness /dark′ nəs/ *n.* Lack of light: *Do not be afraid of the darkness.*

dart /därt/ *v.* Move suddenly and quickly: *The deer darted away.* —*n.* A slender, pointed weapon thrown by hand or shot.

daughter /dô′ ter/ *n.* Female child: *A girl is the daughter of her mother and father.*

dead /ded/ *adj.* **1.** Without life. **2.** Dull: *a dead party.* **3.** Straight: *dead ahead.*

death /deth/ *n.* Dying; the ending of life in people, animals, and plants.

Dec. *abbrev.* for *December.*

December /dē sem′ bər/ *n.* The twelfth and last month of the year, following November. December has 31 days.

declare /dē klãr′/ *v.* Say; make known. **declared, declaring.**

deep /dēp/ *adj.* **1.** Far down from the surface. **2.** Going a long way back from the front: *a deep tunnel.* **3.** Low in pitch: *a deep voice.* **4.** Earnest: *deep feeling.* **5.** Making you take much time in thinking: *a deep subject.*

degree /də grē′/ *n.* **1.** A step in a scale; stage in a process: *By degrees she became a good skater.* **2.** Amount: *To what degree are you interested in reading?* **3.** Unit for measurement of temperature.

deliver /dē liv′ ər/ *v.* **1.** Carry and give out: *She delivers our paper each evening.* **2.** Hand over. **3.** Rescue; save: *A passing ship delivered the shipwrecked passengers.*

demand /dē mand′/ *v.* **1.** Ask for as a right. **2.** Ask for with authority. **3.** Need: *A puppy demands attention.* —*n.* **1.** Claim: *demands upon one's time.* **2.** Call; request: *The demand for apples is great in the fall.*

depend /dē pend′/ *v.* **1.** Have as a support; get help from. **2.** Rely; trust. **3.** Be a result of: *The success of the picnic depends on the weather.*

desert¹ /dez′ ərt/ *n.* Region without trees and water. —*adj.* Barren; not inhabited: *a desert island.*

desert² /də zėrt′/ *v.* Forsake; go away and leave a person or a place, especially one that should not be left.

despair /də spãr′/ *n.* Loss of hope. —*v.* Lose or be without hope.

dessert /də zėrt′/ *n.* Sweet food served at the end of a meal.

dial /dī′ əl/ *n.* **1.** Marked surface on which a moving pointer shows how much there is of something. **2.** Plate or disk of a radio or television set with numbers and letters on it for tuning in to a radio or television station. **3.** Part of an automatic telephone used in making telephone calls. —*v.* **1.** Tune in by using a radio or television dial. **2.** Call by means of a telephone dial.

diamond /dī′ mənd/ *or* /dī′ ə mənd/ *n.* **1.** Colorless or tinted precious stone, formed of pure carbon in crystals. Diamond is the hardest substance known. **2.** Figure shaped like this: ◆ . **3.** Space inside the lines that connect the bases in baseball.

diet /dī′ ət/ *n.* **1.** The usual kind of food and

/a/ ran /ā/ rain /ã/ care /ä/ car /e/ hen /ē/ he /ėr/ her /i/ in /ī/ ice /o/ not /ō/ no /ô/ off /u/ us
/ū/ use /ü/ tool /ů/ took /ou/ cow /oi/ boy /ch/ church /hw/ when /ng/ sing /sh/ ship /ᵺ/ this
/th/ thin /zh/ vision /ə/ about, taken, pencil, lemon, circus

drink. **2.** Special food eaten in sickness, or to make oneself fat or thin. —*v.* Eat special food as part of a doctor's treatment, or to make oneself fat or thin.

difference /dif′ ər əns/ *n.* **1.** Being different. **2.** The result of subtracting: *The difference between 6 and 10 is 4.* **3.** A dispute.

different /dif′ ər ənt/ *adj.* **1.** Not alike: *different names.* **2.** Separate; distinct: *three different times.* **3.** Unusual.

difficult /dif′ ə kult/ *adj.* **1.** Hard to do: *a difficult job.* **2.** Hard to control: *a difficult child.*

dine /dīn/ *v.* Eat dinner. **dined, dining.**

direct /də rekt′/ *v.* **1.** Manage; guide. **2.** Order. **3.** Show the way. —*adj.* **1.** Without a turn; straight. **2.** Frank; truthful: *a direct answer.*

dis— *prefix.* The opposite of; not: *distrust.*

disagree /dis′ ə grē′/ *v.* **1.** Fail to agree. **2.** Differ. **3.** Quarrel. **4.** Be harmful: *Strawberries disagree with me.* **disagreed, disagreeing.**

disappear /dis′ ə pir′/ *v.* Pass from sight; pass from existence.

disappoint /dis′ ə point′/ *v.* **1.** Fail to satisfy one's desire, wish, or hope. **2.** Fail to keep a promise to.

discover /dis kuv′ ər/ *v.* See or learn of for the first time.

disease /də zēz′/ *n.* Sickness; illness.

dislike /dis līk′/ *v.* Not like. —*n.* A feeling of not liking. **disliked, disliking.**

distrust /dis trust′/ *v.* Not trust; doubt. —*n.* Lack of trust; lack of belief in the goodness of.

disturb /dis tėrb′/ *v.* **1.** Destroy the peace, quiet, or rest of. **2.** Put out of order. **3.** Make uneasy.

divide /də vīd′/ *v.* **1.** Separate into parts. **2.** Share. **3.** Disagree: *The school divided on the choice of a motto.* **divided, dividing.**

dizzy /diz′ ē/ *adj.* **1.** Likely to fall, stagger, or spin around; not steady. **2.** Confused. **dizzier, dizziest.**

do /dü/ *v.* Act; carry out: *do work.* **did, done, doing.**

doctor /dok′ tər/ *n.* Person who knows how to treat diseases; dentist.

does /duz/ *v. See* **do.** *She does her work well.*

doesn't /duz′ ənt/ Does not.

dollar /dol′ ər/ *n.* Unit of money in the United States. 100 cents make one dollar.

—dom *suffix* used to form nouns. **1.** Position, rank, or realm of a ____: *Kingdom* means *realm of a king.* **2.** Condition of being ____: *Freedom* means *condition of being free.*

doubt /dout/ *v.* Not believe; feel unsure or uncertain. —*n.* Uncertain state of mind.

downstairs /doun′ stãrz′/ *or* /doun′ stãrz′/ *n.* Lower floor. —*adj.* On the lower floor: *the downstairs rooms.* —*adv.* On or to a lower floor: *She ran downstairs.*

downtown /doun′ toun′/ *adv.* To or in the main part of a town: *Mother has gone downtown shopping.*

doz. *abbrev.* for *dozen.*

doze /dōz/ *n.* A light sleep; nap. —*v.* Sleep lightly. **dozed, dozing.**

dozen /duz′ ən/ *n.* 12; group of 12. *pl.* **dozens** *or* **dozen.**

Dr. *abbrev.* for *doctor.* *pl.* **Drs.**

drag /drag/ *v.* **1.** Pull or draw along the ground. **2.** Go too slowly. **dragged, dragging.** —*n.* Anything that holds something back: *A lazy player is a drag on the team.*

draw /drô/ *v.* **1.** Pull: *draw a wagon.* **2.** Move: *draw near.* **3.** Attract: *draw a crowd.* **4.** Make a picture with a pencil, pen, or chalk. **drew, drawn, drawing.**

drew /drü/ *v. See* **draw.**

dried /drīd/ *v. See* **dry.**

dry /drī/ *adj.* **1.** Not wet. **2.** Empty of water or other liquid. **3.** Not interesting: *a dry book.* **4.** Without butter: *dry toast.* **drier, driest.** —*v.* Make or become dry. **dried, drying.**

dumb /dum/ *adj.* Not able to speak.

dump /dump/ *v.* Empty out.

duty /dü′ tē/ *or* /dü′ tē/ *n.* **1.** The thing that is right to do; what one ought to do. **2.** Things that one has to do in his or her work. **3.** Tax on taking articles out of or bringing them into a country. *pl.* **duties.**

Ee

eagle /ē′ gəl/ *n.* Large bird that can see far and fly strongly: *The bald eagle is the symbol of the United States.*

eardrum /ir′ drum′/ *n.* Thin membrane across the middle ear that vibrates when sound waves strike it.

early /ėr′ lē/ *adj.* **1.** In the first part: *The early part of the day is cool.* **2.** Before the usual time: *an early dinner.* **earlier, earliest.** —*adv.* Before the usual time: *Come early.*

ear-syllables /ir′ sil′ ə bəlz/ *n.* The word parts we hear.

earthquake /ėrth′ kwāk′/ *n.* Shaking of the ground, caused by the sudden movement of rock far beneath the earth's surface.

east /ēst/ *n.* **1.** Direction of the sunrise. **2.** The eastern part of a country. —*adj.* Coming from the east: *an east wind.* —*adv.* Toward the east: *Go east to find the road.*

echo /ek′ō/ *n.* Sounding again. *pl.* **echoes.** —*v.* **1.** Be heard again. **2.** Say again or do always what another says or does. **echoed, echoing.**

either /ē′ ᴛнᴇr/ *or* /ī′ ᴛнᴇr/ *adj.* **1.** One or the other of two: *Either girl may stay.* **2.** Each of two: *There are houses on either side of the street.* —*adv.* Any more than another: *I don't like that either.*

electric /ē lek′ trik/ *adj.* Of electricity; having something to do with electricity.

elegant /el′ ə gənt/ *adj.* Refined or tastefully lavish; luxurious: *an elegant restaurant.*

elephant /el′ ə fənt/ *n.* The largest four-footed animal now living. It has a long snout called a trunk.

—ence *suffix* used to form nouns. Quality or act of being ____ent: *Absence* means *act or fact of being absent.*

enchant /en chant′/ *v.* **1.** Use magic on; put under a spell. **2.** Please greatly; charm: *The music enchanted the children.*

enemy /en′ ə mē/ *n.* **1.** One who is on the other side or against; not a friend. **2.** Anything that will harm: *Frost is an enemy of flowers. pl.* **enemies.**

engine /en′ jən/ *n.* **1.** Machine for applying power to some work, especially a machine that can start others moving. **2.** Machine that pulls a railroad train.

enough /ə nuf′/ *adj.* As much or as many as needed: *enough food.* —*n.* As much as needed: *enough to eat.* —*adv.* Until no more is needed or wanted: *Have you played enough?*

—ent *suffix* used to form adjectives or nouns. *adj.* ____ing: *Different* means *differing.* —*n.* One who ____s: *Student* means *one who studies.*

envy /en′ vē/ *n.* Ill will at another's good fortune. —*v.* Feel envy toward. **envied, envying.**

equal /ē′ kwəl/ *adj.* The same in amount, size, number, or rank. —*v.* Be the same as. —*n.* Person or thing that is equal.

escape /ə skāp′/ *v.* **1.** Get free. **2.** Keep safe from: *We escaped the measles.* **escaped, escaping.** —*n.* Act or way of escaping.

etc. *abbrev.* for *and so forth.*

except /ek sept′/ *prep.* Leaving out: *She works every day except Sunday.* —*v.* Leave out: *Those who did excellent work were excepted from the test.* —*conj.* But: *I would have had a perfect score, except I missed the last question.*

excuse /eks kūz′/ *v.* Forgive; pardon: *Excuse me, please.* **excused, excusing.** /eks kūs′/ —*n.* A reason that is given: *I have an excuse for being late.*

exercise /ek′ sər sīz/ *n.* **1.** Use; practice. **2.** Something that gives practice: *the exercises at the end of the lesson.* —*v.* **1.** Make use of: *exercise caution in crossing the street.* **2.** Take exercise. **exercised, exercising.**

eye-syllables /ī′ sil′ ə bəlz/ *n.* The word parts we see to study the spelling of a word.

Ff

factory /fak′ tər ē/ *n.* Building or group of buildings where things are manufactured. *pl.* **factories.**

fail /fāl/ *v.* **1.** Not succeed; not be able to do. **2.** Not do: *He failed to follow our advice.* **3.** Die away: *The sick man's heart failed.*

famous /fā′ məs/ *adj.* Very well-known.

fan /fan/ *n.* Instrument with which to stir the air in order to cool a room or one's face, or to blow dust away. —*v.* **1.** Stir the air; blow on; stir up: *Fan the fire.* **2.** Use a fan on: *She fanned herself.* **fanned, fanning.**

fancy /fan′ sē/ *adj.* Decorated. **fancier, fanciest.** —*n.* **1.** Something imagined: *Is it a fancy, or do I hear a sound?* **2.** Liking: *a fancy for bright colors. pl.* **fancies.** —*v.* Picture to oneself; imagine. **fancied, fancying.**

farewell /fãr′ wel′/ *n.* Good-by. —*adj.* Parting; last: *They gave the farewell performance last week.*

farther /fär′ ᴛнᴇr/ *adv.* More far: *We walked farther than we meant to.* —*adj.* More far: *The farther tree is beside his house.*

faultless /fôlt′ ləs/ *adj.* Without a fault; perfect.

favor /fā′ vər/ *n.* Act of kindness. —*v.* **1.** Show kindness to: *Favor us with a song.* **2.** Like: *favor her plan.* **3.** Give more than is fair to: *The teacher favors that boy.* **4.** Look like.

favorite /fā′ vər ət/ *adj.* Liked better than

/a/ ran /ā/ rain /ã/ care /ä/ car /e/ hen /ē/ he /ėr/ her /i/ in /ī/ ice /o/ not /ō/ no /ô/ off /u/ us /ū/ use /ü/ tool /ù/ took /ou/ cow /oi/ boy /ch/ church /hw/ when /ng/ sing /sh/ ship /ᴛн/ this /th/ thin /zh/ vision /ə/ about, taken, pencil, lemon, circus

others. *—n.* Person or thing liked very much: *She is a favorite with everyone.*

Feb. *abbrev.* for *February.*

February /feb′ rü er′ ē/ *n.* The second month of the year, following January. February has 28 days except in leap years when it has 29 days.

few /fū/ *adj.* Not many. *—n.* Small number.

field /fēld/ *n.* **1.** Land with few or no trees. **2.** Land used for crops or pasture. **3.** Piece of land used for special purpose: *baseball field.* *—v.* (in baseball) Stop or catch a batted ball.

fierce /firs/ *adj.* Savage; wild. **fiercer, fiercest.**

firm¹ /fėrm/ *adj.* **1.** Solid; not easily moved. **2.** Positive: *a firm voice.*

firm² /fėrm/ *n.* Company of two or more persons in business together.

flap /flap/ *n.* **1.** Piece hanging or fastened at one edge only: *His coat has flaps on the pockets.* **2.** A flapping motion or flapping noise. *—v.* **1.** Strike noisily with something broad and flat. **2.** Swing about loosely and with some noise. **flapped, flapping.**

flat¹ /flat/ *adj.* **1.** Smooth and level; even: *flat land.* **2.** Not deep or thick: *A plate is flat.* **flatter, flattest.**

flat² /flat/ *n.* Apartment or set of rooms on one floor.

flavor /flā′ vər/ *n.* Taste. *—v.* Season: *We use salt to flavor vegetables.*

flock /flok/ *n.* **1.** Group of animals of one kind herded together. **2.** Crowd: *a flock of visitors.* *—v.* **1.** Go in a flock. **2.** Come crowding.

fold /fōld/ *v.* Bend or double over on itself: *fold a letter.* *—n.* Layer of something folded: *a fold of cotton.*

foot /fût/ *n.* **1.** End part of the leg. **2.** Part opposite the head of something. **3.** Bottom. **4.** Measure of length; 12 inches. *pl.* **feet.**

football /fût′ bôl′/ *n.* **1.** Game played with a leather ball which is to be carried or kicked past the goal line at the end of the field. **2.** Ball used in this game.

footprint /fût′ print′/ *n.* Mark made by a foot.

forecast /fôr′ kast′/ *v.* Tell what is coming: *Cool weather is forecast for next week.* *—n.* Statement of what is coming: *the weather forecast.*

forenoon /fôr′ nün′/ *n.* Time of morning before noon.

forest /fôr′ əst/ *n.* Thick woods; woodland often covering many miles. *—adj.* Of the forest: *forest fires.* *—v.* Plant with forest trees.

fork /fôrk/ *n.* **1.** Instrument with a handle and two or more long, pointed parts at one end, used for eating. **2.** Instrument used to lift and throw, such as a pitchfork. **3.** Anything shaped like a fork: *a fork in the road.* *—v.* Lift, throw, or dig with a fork: *fork hay into a wagon.*

forward /fôr′ wərd/ *adj.* Bold: *Don't be so forward as to interrupt the speaker.* *—adv.* Ahead: *move forward.* *—v.* Send on farther: *forward the mail.*

fountain /foun′ tən/ *n.* **1.** Spring of water. **2.** Place to get a drink: *a drinking fountain.*

Fri. *abbrev.* for *Friday.*

Friday /frī′ dā/ *n.* The sixth day of the week, following Thursday.

fright /frīt/ *n.* Sudden fear.

frost /frôst/ *n.* Moisture frozen on or in a surface: *On cold mornings there is frost on the glass.* *—v.* Cover with frost or anything that suggests frost: *frost the drink; frost a cake.*

ft. *abbrev.* for **1.** Foot. **2.** Feet.

fuel /fū′ əl/ *n.* Anything that can be burned to make a useful fire.

—ful *suffix* used to form adjectives or nouns. *adj.* **1.** Full of ___: *Cheerful* means *full of cheer.* **2.** Showing ___: *Careful* means *showing care.* *—n.* Enough to fill a ___: *Cupful* means *enough to fill a cup.*

furious /fūr′ ē əs/ *adj.* **1.** Full of wild anger: *He was furious when I broke the bat.* **2.** Violent; raging: *A tornado is a furious storm.* **3.** Of unchecked energy, speed, etc.: *furious activity.*

furnace /fėr′ nəs/ *n.* Something to make a hot fire in. A furnace has a hot box or enclosed chamber for the fire.

future /fū′ chər/ *n.* Time to come; what is to come. *—adj.* Coming: *your future years.*

Gg

gain /gān/ *v.* Get; obtain. *—n.* Advantage; what one gains.

gal. *abbrev.* for *gallon.* *pl.* **gal. or gals.**

gallon /gal′ ən/ *n.* Measure for liquids equal to 4 quarts.

garage /gə räzh′/ *n.* **1.** Place where automobiles are kept. **2.** Shop for repairing automobiles.

garbage /gär′ bij/ *n.* Scraps of food to be thrown away.

geese /gēs/ *n.* Plural of **goose.**

germ /jėrm/ *n.* **1.** Animal or plant, too small to be seen without a microscope. **2.** Earliest form of any living thing; seed; bud.

ghost /gōst/ *n.* Spirit of one who is dead appearing to the living.

giant /jī′ ənt/ *n.* **1.** Imaginary being like a huge man. **2.** Person of great size. —*adj.* Huge.

glare /glãr/ *n.* **1.** A strong bright light. **2.** Fierce, angry stare. —*v.* **1.** Give off a strong, bright light. **2.** Stare fiercely and angrily. **glared, glaring.**

glove /gluv/ *n.* Covering for the hand with separate places for each finger and the thumb. —*v.* Cover with a glove. **gloved, gloving.**

glue /glü/ *n.* Sticky substance used to stick things together. —*v.* **1.** Stick together with glue. **2.** Fasten tightly. **glued, gluing.**

go /gō/ *v.* **1.** Move along. **2.** Move away; leave. **3.** Be in motion or action; act; work; run: *Make the washing machine go.* **went, gone, going.**

gone /gôn/ *adj.* **1.** Left. **2.** Used up: *The food is gone.* —*v.* See **go.** *They have gone away.*

goose /güs/ *n.* **1.** Wild or tame swimming bird, like a duck, but larger and having a longer neck. **2.** A silly person. *pl.* **geese.**

gown /goun/ *n.* **1.** Woman's dress. **2.** Loose outer garment worn by college graduates, lawyers, and others.

grateful /grāt′ fəl/ *adj.* Thankful.

great /grāt/ *adj.* **1.** Big; large. **2.** Much: *great pain.* **3.** Famous: *a great woman.*

greedy /grē′ dē/ *adj.* Wanting to get more than one's share. **greedier, greediest.**

green /grēn/ *n.* The color of most growing plants, grass, and leaves in summer. —*adj.* **1.** Having this color. **2.** Not ripe; not fully grown.

grip /grip/ *n.* **1.** Small suitcase. **2.** Tight grasp. —*v.* Take a firm hold on. **gripped, gripping.**

groan /grōn/ *n.* Deep, short moan. —*v.* **1.** Give a groan or groans. **2.** Be loaded: *The table groaned with food.*

grocery /grō′ sər ē/ *n.* Store that sells food and household supplies. *pl.* **groceries.**

grow /grō/ *v.* **1.** Become bigger; increase. **2.** Become: *It grew colder.* **grew, grown, growing.**

grown /grōn/ *v.* See **grow.** *He has grown tall.*

grown-up /grōn′ up′/ *adj.* Adult: *a grown-up person.* —*n.* Adult: *The boy eats like a grown-up.*

grunt /grunt/ *n.* **1.** The deep, hoarse sound that a hog makes. **2.** Sound like the grunt of a hog. —*v.* Make this sound.

guard /gärd/ *v.* **1.** Watch over; keep safe. **2.** Keep from escaping. —*n.* **1.** Person or group that guards. **2.** Anything that gives protection: *A fender is a guard against mud.*

Hh

habit /hab′ it/ *n.* **1.** Custom; practice. **2.** The dress of persons belonging to a religious order: *Many monks and nuns wear habits.*

hadn't /had′ ənt/ Had not.

hall /hôl/ *n.* **1.** Way for going through a building. **2.** Large room for holding meetings or parties.

halt /hôlt/ *v.* Stop for a time. —*n.* A stop.

handkerchief /hang′ kər chif/ *n.* Soft square of cloth used for wiping the nose, face, or hands.

happiness /hap′ ē nəs/ *n.* **1.** Being happy; gladness. **2.** Good luck; good fortune.

hasn't /haz′ ənt/ Has not.

hate /hāt/ *v.* Dislike very much. **hated, hating.** —*n.* Very strong dislike: *She felt hate for her enemies.*

haul /hôl/ *v.* **1.** Pull or drag. **2.** Carry; transport. —*n.* Amount won or taken at one time: *the haul taken by the fishing boats.*

haunt /hônt/ *v.* **1.** Visit often: *People say ghosts haunt that house.* **2.** Be often with: *Memories of his past haunt the old man.*

have /hav/ *v.* **1.** Hold in one's keeping: *have a new house.* **2.** Be forced: *have to sleep.* **3.** Experience: *have fun.* **4.** Know: *have an idea.* **has, had, having.**

hawk /hôk/ *n.* Bird of prey with a strong, hooked beak, long claws, broad wings, and keen sight. —*v.* Hunt with trained hawks.

health /helth/ *n.* Being well; freedom from illness of any kind.

heavy /hev′ ē/ *adj.* **1.** Hard to lift; having much weight. **2.** Large; greater than usual: *a heavy rain; a heavy crop.* **3.** Hard to endure: *heavy sorrow.* **4.** Weighted down: *heavy heart; heavy eyes.* **heavier, heaviest.**

he's /hēz/ He is.

history /his′ tər ē/ *n.* **1.** Story or record of important past events that happened to a person or nation: *the history of the United States.* **2.** The known past: *This ship has a great history. pl.* **histories.**

hobby /hob′ ē/ *n.* Something a person likes to work at or study which is not his or her main business: *Growing roses is his hobby. pl.* **hobbies.**

homemade /hōm′ mād′/ *adj.* Made at home.

/a/ ran　/ā/ rain　/ã/ care　/ä/ car　/e/ hen　/ē/ he　/ėr/ her　/i/ in　/ī/ ice　/o/ not　/ō/ no　/ô/ off　/u/ us
/ū/ use　/ü/ tool　/u̇/ took　/ou/ cow　/oi/ boy　/ch/ church　/hw/ when　/ng/ sing　/sh/ ship　/ŦH/ this
/th/ thin　/zh/ vision　/ə/ about, taken, pencil, lemon, circus

homesick /hōm′ sik′/ *adj.* Overcome by sadness because home is far away; longing for home.

homograph /hom′ ə graf′/ *n.* One of two or more words that have the same spelling but different meanings, such as **root** (for a team) and **root** (of a tree).

homonym /hom′ ə nim′/ *n.* One of two or more words that sound alike but have different meanings and spellings, such as **to, too,** and **two.**

Hon. *abbrev.* for *Honorable.*

honest /on′ əst/ *adj.* **1.** Fair and upright; truthful. **2.** Not hiding one's real nature: *an honest face.* **3.** Pure; not mixed with something of less worth: *honest value.*

honor /on′ ər/ *n.* Glory; fame; good name. —*v.* Respect; think highly of.

honorable /on′ ər ə bəl/ *adj.* **1.** Worthy; noble. **2. Honorable,** title of respect: *the Honorable John Jones.*

hoof /hůf/ *n.* Hard covering on the feet of horses, cattle, sheep, pigs, and some other animals. *pl.* **hoofs** or **hooves.**

horn /hôrn/ *n.* **1.** Hard growth on the heads of cattle and some other animals. **2.** The substance or material of horns. **3.** Musical instrument. **4.** Device sounded as a warning signal: *an automobile horn.*

hospital /hos′ pi təl/ *n.* Place for the care of the sick or injured.

hotel /hō tel′/ *n.* House or large building that supplies rooms and food for pay to travelers and others.

howl /houl/ *v.* Give a long, loud, mournful cry. —*n.* A long, loud mournful cry: *Our dog may howl at night.*

huge /hūj/ *adj.* Very, very large. **huger, hugest.**

hum /hum/ *n.* A continuous murmuring sound: *hum of bees; hum of the city streets.* —*v.* **1.** Make a continuous murmuring sound. **2.** Sing with closed lips, not sounding words. **hummed, humming.**

human /hū′ mən/ *n.* Person. —*adj.* **1.** Belonging to people: *The history of America has human interest.* **2.** Having the form or qualities of people: *The monkey looks almost human. Men and woman are human beings.*

humor /hū′ mər/ *n.* **1.** Funny or amusing quality. **2.** State of mind; temper: *good humor.* —*v.* Give in to the whims of a person: *The parents were told to humor the sick child.*

hydrant /hī′ drənt/ *n.* Large, upright pipe with a valve for drawing water from a water main.

Ii

—ible *suffix* used to form *adjectives.* Can be ____ed: *Perfectible* means *can be perfected.*

iceberg /īs′ bėrg′/ *n.* Large mass of ice floating in the sea.

idea /ī dē′ ə/ *n.* **1.** Belief, plan, or picture in the mind. **2.** Opinion: *I had no idea school could be so pleasant.*

imagine /i maj′ ən/ *v.* Form a picture in the mind; have an idea. **imagined, imagining.**

important /im pôrt′ ənt/ *adj.* Meaning very much; having value or influence: *an important meeting; an important person.*

in. *abbrev.* for *inch.*

inch /inch/ *n.* Measure of length; $\frac{1}{12}$ of a foot. *pl.* **inches.**

infant /in′ fənt/ *n.* Baby —*adj.* **1.** For an infant. **2.** In an early stage.

instant /in′ stənt/ *n.* **1.** A particular moment: *Stop talking this instant.* **2.** Moment of time. —*adj.* **1.** Without delay: *instant relief.* **2.** Prepared beforehand and requiring little or no additional cooking: *instant pudding.*

instead /in sted′/ *adv.* In another's place.

interest /in′ tər əst/ *or* /in′ trəst/ *n.* **1.** Feeling of wanting to know, see, do, or share in: *an interest in sports.* **2.** Power to arouse such feeling: *A dull book lacks interest.* **3.** Share in property, business: *an interest in the company.* **4.** Money paid for the use of money. **5.** Benefit: *She looks after the interest of her family.* —*v.* **1.** Arouse a feeling of wanting to know, see, do, or share in. **2.** Cause a person to take part in.

interj. *abbrev.* for *interjection.*

interjection /in′ tər jek′ shən/ *n.* A word that is used as an exclamation, often expressing surprise, shock, etc., such as *Oh!* in *"Oh! You stepped on my foot!"*

into /in′ tü/ *prep.* **1.** To the inside of; toward and inside: *Come into the house.* **2.** So as to become; to the form of: *Divide the apple into three parts.*

—ious *suffix* used to form *adjectives.* Having ____; having much ____; full of ____: *Anxious* means *having anxiety or fearful concern.*

iron /ī′ ərn/ *n.* **1.** The commonest and most useful metal from which tools and machinery are made. **2.** Implement with a flat surface to press clothing. —*adj.* Made of iron: *an iron fence.* —*v.* Press with a heated iron.

island /ī′ lənd/ *n.* Body of land surrounded by water.

its /its/ *adj.* Belonging to it: *The dog wagged its tail.*

it's /its/ **1.** It is. **2.** It has.

Jj

jacket /jak′ ət/ *n.* A short coat.

Jan. *abbrev.* for *January.*

January /jan′ ū er′ ē/ *n.* The first month of the year. January has 31 days.

jealous /jel′ əs/ *adj.* **1.** Fearful that somebody you love may prefer someone else. **2.** Full of envy.

jelly /jel′ ē/ *n.* Food made by boiling fruit juices and sugar or by using some stiffening substance like gelatin. *pl.* **jellies.** —*v.* Become jelly; turn into jelly. **jellied, jellying.**

jigsaw /jig′ sô/ *n.* Narrow saw mounted in a frame and worked with an up-and-down motion, used to cut curves.

joyous /joi′ əs/ *adj.* Joyful; glad.

juice /jüs/ *n.* **1.** Liquid part of fruits, vegetables, and meat. **2.** Liquids in the body: *the juices of the stomach.*

July /jü lī′/ *n.* The seventh month of the year, following June. July has 31 days.

June /jün/ *n.* The sixth month of the year, following May. June has 30 days.

justice /jus′ təs/ *n.* Fair dealing; fairness.

Kk

kettle /ket′ əl/ *n.* Any metal cooking container, usually having a handle and spout.

kneel /nēl/ *v.* Go down on one's knee or knees. **knelt** or **kneeled, kneeling.**

knight /nīt/ *n.* **1.** In the Middle Ages, a man raised to an honorable rank and bound to do good deeds. **2.** In modern times, a man raised to an honorable rank because of great achievements or service.

knit /nit/ *v.* **1.** Make with long needles out of yarn. **2.** Grow together: *A broken bone knits.* **3.** Wrinkle: *She knits her brow.*

know /nō/ *v.* **1.** Have the facts of. **2.** Be acquainted with: *I know him very well.* **knew, known, knowing.**

known /nōn/ *v.* See **know.** *She has known plants like these.*

Ll

label /lā′ bəl/ *n.* Paper or other material attached to anything and marked to show what or whose it is, or where it is to go. —*v.* Put or write a label on.

lady /lā′ dē/ *n.* **1.** Woman who is looked up to. **2.** Any woman. *pl.* **ladies.**

laid /lād/ *v.* See **lay.** *She laid her bundle on the table.*

lake /lāk/ *n.* Body of water entirely or nearly surrounded by land.

land /land/ *n.* **1.** Ground; soil. **2.** The solid part of the earth: *After weeks at sea, we sighted land.* **3.** Country. —*v.* Go on shore from a boat or ship.

landlord /land′ lôrd′/ *n.* Person who owns buildings or lands that he or she rents to others.

language /lang′ gwij/ *n.* **1.** Human speech, written or spoken. **2.** The speech of one nation or group. **3.** Wording; words: *the language of the contract.* **4.** Form, style, or kind of language.

lay¹ /lā/ *v.* **1.** Put down: *Lay your hat on the table.* **2.** Place: *Lay your hand on your heart.* **3.** Give forth (an egg or eggs). **laid, laying.**

lay² /lā/ *v.* See **lie².** *I lay down to sleep.*

lb. *abbrev.* for *pound.* *pl.* **lbs.**

lemon /lem′ ən/ *n.* A sour, light-yellow fruit that grows in warm climates. —*adj.* Flavored with lemon.

less /les/ *adj.* Smaller. —*adv.* To a smaller degree.

—less *suffix* used to form *adjectives.* **1.** Without ____: *Homeless* means *without a home.* **2.** Does not ____: *Tireless* means *does not tire.*

level /lev′ əl/ *adj.* **1.** Flat; even. **2.** Of equal height: *level with the window.* —*n.* **1.** Instrument for showing whether a surface is level. **2.** Height: *a level of 60 feet.* —*v.* Make level.

lever /lev′ ər/ *or* /lē′ vər/ *n.* **1.** Bar for raising or moving a weight at one end by pushing down at the other end. It must be supported at any point in between. **2.** Any bar working on an axis or support.

liar /lī′ ər/ *n.* Person who tells lies.

library /lī′ brer′ ē/ *n.* **1.** A collection of books. **2.** Room or building in which books are kept. *pl.* **libraries.**

/a/ ran /ā/ rain /ã/ care /ä/ car /e/ hen /ē/ he /ėr/ her /i/ in /ī/ ice /o/ not /ō/ no /ô/ off /u/ us
/ū/ use /ü/ tool /ů/ took /ou/ cow /oi/ boy /ch/ church /hw/ when /ng/ sing /sh/ ship /ᴛH/ this
/th/ thin /zh/ vision /ə/ about, taken, pencil, lemon, circus

lie¹ /lī/ *v.* Speak falsely. **lied, lying.** —*n.* Statement that is not true.

lie² /lī/ *v.* **1.** Have one's body in a flat position: *lie in bed.* **2.** Be; be placed: *The lake lies to the southeast.* **3.** Rest on a surface. **lay, lain, lying.**

lied /līd/ *v.* See **lie¹**. *He lied about the time he arrived at school.*

limb /lim/ *n.* **1.** Leg, arm, or wing. **2.** Large branch: *the limb of a tree.*

limit /lim′ it/ *n.* The farthest edge; where something ends or must end. —*v.* Set a limit to; restrict.

lion /lī′ ən/ *n.* Large, strong animal of Africa. The male has a full, flowing mane of coarse hair.

listen /lis′ ən/ *v.* Try to hear; attend.

lonely /lōn′ lē/ *adj.* **1.** Feeling oneself alone and longing for company or friends. **2.** Without many people: *a lonely road.* **3.** Alone: *a lonely tree.* **lonelier, loneliest.**

loosen /lü′ sən/ *v.* **1.** Untie; unfasten; make loose or looser: *loosen your collar.* **2.** Become loose or looser.

lose /lüz/ *v.* **1.** Not have any longer. **2.** Fail to win. **3.** Bring to ruin: *The ship and its crew were lost in the storm.* **lost, losing.**

loss /lôs/ *n.* **1.** Person or thing lost: *Their house was a complete loss in the fire.* **2.** Value of thing lost: *The loss from the fire was $10,000.* **3.** Defeat. *pl.* **losses.**

lost /lôst/ *v.* See **lose**. *I lost my pencil.* —*adj.* **1.** No longer possessed: *lost friends.* **2.** Not won. **3.** Hopeless. **4.** Wasted: *lost time.*

lumber¹ /lum′ bər/ *n.* Timber cut into boards or planks and prepared for use.

lumber² /lum′ bər/ *v.* Move heavily and slowly: *The truck lumbered down the bumpy road.*

Mm

ma'am /mam/ *n.* Madam.

machine /mə shēn′/ *n.* **1.** Arrangement of fixed and moving parts for doing work, each part having some special job to do. **2.** Automobile.

made-up /mād′ up′/ *adj.* Not real or true.

mail /māl/ *n.* **1.** Letters, postcards, papers, and parcels sent by post. **2.** System by which such letters and papers are sent. —*v.* Send by mail; put in a mailbox.

male /māl/ *n.* Man or boy. —*adj.* **1.** Having to do with men or boys. **2.** Belonging to the sex that can father young: *A rooster is a male bird.*

manage /man′ ij/ *v.* Control; handle; conduct; direct. **managed, managing.**

mankind /man′ kīnd′/ *n.* All human beings.

Mar. *abbrev.* for *March.*

March /märch/ *n.* The third month of the year, following February. March has 31 days.

market /mär′ kət/ *n.* Store or place for selling food, cattle, or other things. —*v.* Buy or sell in a market.

marry /mar′ ē/ *v.* **1.** Join as husband and wife. **2.** Take as husband or wife. **3.** Become married. **married, marrying.**

May /mā/ *n.* The fifth month of the year, following April. May has 31 days.

meal¹ /mēl/ *n.* Food eaten or served at any one time.

meal² /mēl/ *n.* **1.** Grain ground up: *corn meal.* **2.** Anything ground to a powder.

mean /mēn/ *v.* Have in mind. **meant, meaning.** —*adj.* **1.** Unkind. **2.** Bad-tempered.

meant /ment/ *v.* See **mean**. *She explained what she meant.*

measure /mezh′ ər/ *v.* **1.** Find the size or amount of anything. **2.** Mark off in inches, feet, quarts, or some other unit. **3.** Be of a certain size or amount: *The paper measures 8 × 10 inches.* **measured, measuring.** —*n.* **1.** Size or amount: *His waist measure is 30 inches.* **2.** Something with which to measure. **3.** System of measurement. **4.** A proposed law. **5.** Bar of music.

medal /med′ əl/ *n.* Piece of metal like a coin, with an inscription stamped on it.

medicine /med′ ə sən/ *n.* **1.** Substance used to cure, treat, or prevent disease. **2.** Treatment of diseases or sickness: *The doctor studied medicine for a number of years.*

mend /mend/ *v.* **1.** Put in good condition again; fix. **2.** Improve: *He should mend his manners.* —*n.* A place that has been mended.

—ment *suffix* used to form *nouns.* **1.** Act of ____ing: *Enjoyment* means *act of enjoying.* **2.** State of being ____ed: *Settlement* means *state of being settled.*

merchant /mėr′ chənt/ *n.* Person who buys and sells; storekeeper. —*adj.* Trading; having something to do with trade: *merchant ships.*

message /mes′ ij/ *n.* **1.** Words sent from one person to another. **2.** An official speech or writing: *the President's message.*

metal /met′ əl/ *n.* Substance such as iron, gold, silver, copper, etc. —*adj.* Made of metal: *a metal box.*

mi. *abbrev.* for *mile.*

midnight /mid′ nīt′/ *n.* Twelve o'clock at night.

mile /mīl/ *n.* A distance equal to 5,280 feet.

minus /mī' nəs/ *prep.* **1.** Less; decrease by: *12 minus 3 leaves 9.* **2.** Lacking: *a book minus its cover.* —*adj.* Less than: *A mark of B minus is not so high as a mark of B.* —*n.* The sign – meaning that the quantity following it is to be subtracted. *pl.* **minuses.**

minute[1] /min' ət/ *n.* **1.** One of the 60 equal periods of time that make up an hour; 60 seconds. **2.** A short time; an instant.

minute[2] /mī nüt'/ *adj.* Very, very small; tiny.

Miss /mis/ Title given to a girl or to a woman who is not married: *Miss Brown.*

mistake /mə stāk'/ *n.* Error; blunder; misunderstanding of a thing's meaning. —*v.* **1.** Misunderstand what is seen or heard. **2.** Take wrongly: *I mistook that boy for his brother.* **mistook, mistaken, mistaking.**

Mister /mis' tər/ *n.* Sir; a title put before a man's name or the name of his office.

mistress /mis' trəs/ *n.* **1.** Woman at the head of household or school. **2.** Woman who owns or controls: *The dog came when its mistress called. pl.* **mistresses.**

mixture /miks' chər/ *n.* **1.** Something that has been mixed. **2.** Mixing: *The mixture of the paints took several hours.*

model /mod' əl/ *n.* **1.** Small copy: *model of a ship.* **2.** Person who poses for artists and photographers. **3.** Person in a store who wears garments in order to show customers how they look. —*v.* **1.** Make, shape, or fashion. **2.** Follow. **3.** Pose as a model. —*adj.* Just right: *a model child.*

modern /mod' ərn/ *adj.* **1.** Up-to-date; not old-fashioned: *modern views.* **2.** Of the present time: *Television is a modern invention.*

moment /mō' mənt/ *n.* **1.** A very short space of time; instant: *Won't you stay for a moment?* **2.** A particular point of time.

Mon. *abbrev.* for *Monday.*

Monday /mun' dā/ *n.* The second day of the week, following Sunday.

month /munth/ *n.* One of the twelve periods of time into which a year is divided.

moonlight /mün' līt'/ *n.* Light of the moon. —*adj.* Having the light of the moon.

most /mōst/ *adj.* **1.** Greatest in amount, degree, or number. **2.** Almost all: *most of the people.* —*n.* The greatest number or amount.

motor /mō' tər/ *n.* Engine that makes a machine go. —*adj.* Run by motor: *a motor bicycle.* —*v.* Travel by automobile.

mount[1] /mount/ *v.* **1.** Go up; ascend: *mount stairs.* **2.** Get up on: *mount a horse.* **3.** Put on a horse. **4.** Fix in a setting, backing, support, etc.: *mount a picture on cardboard.* —*n.* **1.** Horse provided for riding. **2.** A setting; backing; support: *the mount for a pic'ure.*

mount[2] /mount/ *n.* A very high hill or mountain.

mountain /moun' tən/ *n.* **1.** Very high hill. **2.** Very large heap or pile of anything: *a mountain of rubbish.* —*adj.* Having to do with mountains: *a mountain plant.*

Mr. *or* **Mr** /mis' tər/ *abbrev.* for *Mister.* Title put in front of a man's name or the name of his position: *Mr. Jones; Mr. President.*

Mrs. *or* **Mrs** /mis' iz/ *abbrev.* for *Mistress.* Title put in front of a married woman's name: *Mrs. Jackson.*

Ms. *or* **Ms** /miz/ Title given to a woman: *Ms. Brown.*

mt. *abbrev.* for **1.** Mountain. **2.** Mount.

museum /mū zē' əm/ *n.* Building or rooms in which a collection of objects is kept and displayed.

Nn

N. *or* **n.** *abbrev.* for **1.** North. **2.** (**n.** only) Noun.

nation /nā' shən/ *n.* Group of people occupying the same country, united under the same government, usually speaking the same language.

nature /nā' chər/ *n.* **1.** The world; all things except those made by man. **2.** The regular ways in which things are or act. **3.** Sort; kind: *books of a scientific nature.*

navy /nā' vē/ *n.* All the ships of war of a country, with their men and women and the department that manages them. *pl.* **navies.**

nearby /nir' bī'/ *adj.* Near; close. —*adv.* To a near place; to a close place.

neat /nēt/ *adj.* **1.** Clean and in order: *a neat room.* **2.** Able and willing to keep things in order: *a neat child.* **3.** Clever: *a neat trick.*

necktie /nek' tī'/ *n.* Narrow band worn around the neck, under the collar of a shirt, and tied in front.

/a/ ran /ā/ rain /ä/ care /ä/ car /e/ hen /ē/ he /ėr/ her /i/ in /ī/ ice /o/ not /ō/ no /ô/ off /u/ us
/ū/ use /ü/ tool /u̇/ took /ou/ cow /oi/ boy /ch/ church /hw/ when /ng/ sing /sh/ ship /ᴛʜ/ this
/th/ thin /zh/ vision /ə/ about, taken, pencil, lemon, circus

neither /nē′ ᴛʜər/ or /nī′ ᴛʜər/ adj. Not either: Neither story is true. —pron. Not either: Neither of us can go. —conj. Not either: Neither you nor I can go.

nervous /nėr′ vəs/ adj. **1.** Easily excited or upset. **2.** Restless or uneasy.

—ness suffix used to form nouns. Quality or state of being ____: Happiness means quality or state of being happy.

nest /nest/ n. Structure built by birds, insects, or the like, as a place to lay eggs. —v. Make and use a nest.

newsreel /nūz′ rēl′/ or /nūz′ rēl′/ n. Motion picture showing current events.

nickel /nik′ əl/ n. **1.** Metal that looks like silver and is somewhat like iron. **2.** A United States or Canadian five-cent piece.

no. or **No.** abbrev. for **1.** Number. pl. **nos. 2.** North.

noisy /noiz′ ē/ adj. **1.** Making much noise. **2.** Full of noise: a noisy street. **3.** Having much noise with it. **noisier, noisiest.**

north /nôrth/ n. The direction toward which the compass needle points. —adv. Toward the north: Drive north. —adj. From or in the north: There is a strong north wind.

northwest /nôrth′ west′/ n. **1.** A north and west direction. **2.** Region in the northwest of a country. —adj. Coming from the north and west: a northwest wind. —adv. Toward the northwest: Walk a mile northwest.

note /nōt/ n. **1.** A short letter. **2.** Words or sentences written down to be remembered. **3.** Fame; greatness: Lincoln is a man of note. **4.** A musical sound. —v. **1.** Write down as a thing to remember. **2.** Notice. **noted, noting.**

notebook /nōt′ bůk′/ n. Book in which to write notes of things to be learned or remembered.

nothing /nuth′ ing/ n. **1.** Not anything: Nothing came by mail. **2.** Zero.

notice /nō′ təs/ n. **1.** Attention: A sudden movement caught her notice. **2.** Warning: The whistle blew to give notice of the train's approach. **3.** Large, printed sign giving information or directions. —v. See; give attention to; observe. **noticed, noticing.**

noun /noun/ n. Word used as the name of a person, place, or thing.

Nov. abbrev. for November.

November /nō vem′ bər/ n. The eleventh month of the year, following October. November has 30 days.

number /num′ bər/ n. Word that tells exactly how many.

Oo

oar /ôr/ n. Long pole with a flat end, used in rowing or steering a boat.

obey /ō bā′/ v. **1.** Do what one is told to do. **2.** Follow the orders of.

object /ob′ jəkt/ n. **1.** Thing: A ball is a round object. /əb jekt′/ —v. **1.** Show dislike: He objects to noise. **2.** Give as a reason against something.

ocean /ō′ shən/ n. **1.** The great body of salt water that covers almost three-fourths of the earth's surface. **2.** Any of its four main divisions—the Atlantic, the Pacific, the Arctic, and the Indian oceans. The waters around the Antarctic continent are considered by some to form a separate ocean.

Oct. abbrev. for October.

October /ok tō′ bər/ n. The tenth month of the year, following September. October has 31 days.

odd /od/ adj. **1.** Strange; queer. **2.** Leaving a remainder of 1 when divided by 2: Three and seven are odd numbers. **3.** Extra: odd jobs. **4.** Left over: There is one odd stocking.

offer /ôf′ ər/ v. **1.** Present: offer a gift. **2.** Suggest; propose: offer a plan. —n. An act of offering: an offer to help.

office /ôf′ es/ n. **1.** Room or rooms in which to work. **2.** Position: accept an office in the company. **3.** Work; job.

often /ôf′ ən/ adj. Many times.

oilskin /oil′ skin′/ n. Cloth treated with oil to make it waterproof.

old-time /ōld′ tīm′/ adj. From long ago; not modern: an old-time movie.

once /wuns/ adv. **1.** One time. **2.** Formerly: That huge dog was once a small pup.

only /ōn′ lē/ adj. **1.** One and no more. **2.** Best; finest: She is the only writer for my taste. —adv. Just: He sold only two. —conj. But.

ornament /ôr′ nə mənt/ n. Decoration; something that adds beauty. /ôr′ nə ment/ v. Decorate; add beauty to.

ounce /ouns/ n. Unit of weight, $\frac{1}{16}$ of a pound; very small amount. Abbreviated **oz.**

—ous suffix used to form adjectives. **1.** Having; having much; full of: Famous means having much fame. **2.** Having the nature of: Villainous means having the nature of a villain. **3.** Like: Thunderous means like thunder.

outlaw /out′ lô′/ n. Lawless person; criminal. —v. Make or declare unlawful.

outlook /out′ lŭk′/ *n.* **1.** View: *The room has a pleasant outlook.* **2.** What seems likely to happen: *The outlook for the picnic is not good; it looks as if it will rain.* **3.** Way of thinking about things: *Her outlook is gloomy.*

oven /uv′ ən/ *n.* **1.** An enclosed space usually in a stove or near a fireplace for baking food. **2.** A small furnace for heating or drying pottery.

oz. *abbrev.* for *ounce.* *pl.* **oz.** or **ozs.**

Pp

package /pak′ ij/ *n.* Bundle of things wrapped or packed together; parcel. —*v.* Put in a package. **packaged, packaging.**

paddle /pad′ əl/ *n.* Short oar with broad blade at one or both ends, used without resting it against the boat. —*v.* **1.** Move a boat or canoe with a paddle. **2.** Spank. **paddled, paddling.**

pain /pān/ *n.* Feeling of being hurt; suffering. —*v.* Cause to suffer: *Does your tooth pain you?*

pair /pãr/ *n.* **1.** Set of two; two that go together. **2.** Single thing that consists of two parts that cannot be used separately: *pair of scissors.* —*v.* Arrange in pairs.

pane /pān/ *n.* Single sheet of glass in a division of a window, a door, or a sash.

pare /pãr/ *v.* Cut, trim, or shave off the outer part of; peel. **pared, paring.**

parent /pãr′ ənt/ *n.* **1.** Father or mother. **2.** Any animal or plant that produces offspring.

pass /pas/ *v.* **1.** Go by. **2.** Move on: *The time passed slowly.* **3.** Hand around. **4.** Use or spend: *pass time.* **5.** Move: *Pass your hand over this cloth.* **passed, passed** or **past, passing.** —*n.* **1.** Written permission. **2.** A free ticket. **3.** Narrow road or path. *pl.* **passes.**

past /past/ *n.* **1.** Time gone by: *History is a study of the past.* **2.** One's past life or history. **3.** The verb form that shows a happening in the past: *The past of* do *is* did. —*adj.* Gone by; ended: *Summer is past.* —*v.* See **pass.**

pasture /pas′ chər/ *n.* **1.** A grassy field; grassy land used for grazing. **2.** Grass and other growing plants: *These lands afford good pasture.* —*v.* Put cattle, sheep, or horses out to pasture. **pastured, pasturing.**

patient /pā′ shənt/ *n.* Person who is being treated by a doctor. —*adj.* Having patience; showing calmness and willingness to wait.

pause /pôz/ *n.* A brief stop or rest. —*v.* Stop for a time; wait. **paused, pausing.**

peace /pēs/ *n.* **1.** Freedom from war or strife of any kind. **2.** Quiet; calm; stillness.

peak /pēk/ *n.* **1.** The pointed top of a mountain or hill. **2.** The highest point. **3.** The pointed end or top: *the peak of the roof.*

pear /pãr/ *n.* Sweet, juicy fruit.

pedal /ped′ əl/ *n.* Lever worked by the foot. —*v.* Work or use the pedals of.

peddle /ped′ əl/ *v.* Carry from place to place and sell. **peddled, peddling.**

peek /pēk/ *v.* Look quickly and slyly; peep. —*n.* A quick, sly look.

perfect /pėr′ fəkt/ *adj.* With no faults; with no mistakes.

perhaps /pər haps′/ *adv.* Possibly; it may be.

petal /pet′ əl/ *n.* One of the parts of a flower, usually colored.

piano /pē an′ ō/ *n.* Large musical instrument whose tones come from wires. The wires are sounded by hammers that are worked by striking keys on a keyboard. *pl.* **pianos.**

picnic /pik′ nik/ *n.* Pleasure trip, with a meal in the open air. —*v.* Go on such a trip. **picnicked, picnicking.**

picture /pik′ chər/ *n.* **1.** Drawing, painting, portrait, or photograph. **2.** Scene. **3.** Idea: *I have a picture of the problem.* **4.** Something beautiful: *She was a picture in her new dress.* —*v.* **1.** Draw, paint, make into a picture. **2.** Imagine. **3.** Show by words; describe: *picture the scene.* **pictured, picturing.**

piece /pēs/ *n.* **1.** One of the parts into which a thing is broken or divided. **2.** A single composition in art: *a piece of music.* —*v.* Join the pieces of. **pieced, piecing.**

pilot /pī′ lət/ *n.* Person who steers a ship or boat or operates the controls of an aircraft. —*v.* Guide, steer, or operate.

pinch /pinch/ *v.* **1.** Squeeze with thumb and forefinger. **2.** Press so as to hurt. **3.** Be stingy with: *pinch pennies.*

pint /pīnt/ *n.* A unit of measure equal to half a quart.

pirate /pī′ rət/ *n.* Robber on the sea. —*v.* Be a pirate; plunder; rob. **pirated, pirating.**

/a/ ran /ā/ rain /ã/ care /ä/ car /e/ hen /ē/ he /ėr/ her /i/ in /ī/ ice /o/ not /ō/ no /ô/ off /u/ us
/ū/ use /ü/ tool /ù/ took /ou/ cow /oi/ boy /ch/ church /hw/ when /ng/ sing /sh/ ship /ŦH/ this
/th/ thin /zh/ vision /ə/ about, taken, pencil, lemon, circus

pity /pit′ ē/ *n.* Sorrow for the suffering of others. —*v.* Feel pity for. **pitied, pitying.**

pl. *abbrev.* for *plural.*

plain /plān/ *n.* Flat stretch of land: *the western plains.* —*adj.* **1.** Not fancy. **2.** Easy to understand. **3.** All of one color: *plain blue.* **4.** Not pretty. **5.** Simple in manner: *a plain person.* **6.** Frank; honest: *plain talk.*

plane¹ /plān/ *n.* Airplane.

plane² /plān/ *n.* Carpenter's tool with a blade for smoothing wood. —*v.* Smooth wood with a plane. **planed, planing.**

planet /plan′ ət/ *n.* One of the heavenly bodies that move around the sun. Mercury, Venus, the Earth, Mars, Jupiter, Saturn, Uranus, Neptune, and Pluto are planets.

plate /plāt/ *n.* **1.** Flat dish, usually round. **2.** Thin, flat sheet of metal. **3.** (in baseball) Home base. —*v.* Cover with a thin layer of silver, gold, or some other metal. **plated, plating.**

platform /plat′ fôrm/ *n.* **1.** A raised level surface: *We waited on the platform at the railroad station.* **2.** Plan of action or statement of principles of a group.

pleasant /plez′ ənt/ *adj.* **1.** Giving pleasure; pleasing: *a pleasant swim.* **2.** Easy to get along with. **3.** Fair; not stormy.

pleasure /plezh′ ər/ *n.* **1.** Feeling of being pleased; delight; joy. **2.** Cause of joy or delight. **3.** Anything that pleases; sport: *He takes his pleasure in riding.*

plow /plou/ *n.* Farm instrument for cutting the soil and turning it over. —*v.* **1.** Use a plow. **2.** Advance as a plow does, slowly and with effort: *The ship plowed through the waves.*

plum /plum/ *n.* Round, juicy fruit with smooth skin and stone, or pit.

plural /plúr′ əl/ *adj.* More than one in number. —*n.* Form of a word to show that it means more than one: Men *is the plural of* man.

p.m. *or* **P.M.** The time from noon to midnight.

pocket /pok′ ət/ *n.* Small bag sewed into clothing for carrying small articles. —*adj.* **1.** Small enough for a pocket: *pocket camera.* **2.** Meant for a pocket. —*v.* **1.** Put in one's pocket. **2.** Take secretly or dishonestly: *One partner pocketed all the profits.*

poem /pō′ əm/ *n.* Composition in verse; arrangement of words in lines with regularly repeated accents and often with rhyme.

poison /poi′ zən/ *n.* Drug or other substance very dangerous to life and health. —*v.* **1.** Kill or harm by poison. **2.** Have a very harmful effect on: *Lies poison the mind.*

police /pə lēs′/ *n.* Persons whose duty it is to keep order and arrest people who break the law. —*v.* Keep in order. **policed, policing.**

polish /pol′ ish/ *v.* Make smooth and shiny. —*n.* **1.** Substance used to give smoothness or shine. **2.** Smoothness; polished condition: *The polish of the furniture.* pl. **polishes.**

polite /pə līt′/ *adj.* Showing good manners; refined: *a polite person.*

popcorn /pop′ kôrn/ *n.* Kind of corn, the kernels of which burst open and puff out when heated.

porch /pôrch/ *n.* Covered entrance to a building. pl. **porches.**

possible /pos′ ə bəl/ *adj.* **1.** Can be done; can be. **2.** Can be true as a fact.

postscript /pōst′ skript/ *n.* Addition to a letter, written after the letter has been signed.

potato /pə tā′ tō/ *n.* Plant with a starchy tuber used as a vegetable. This vegetable is round or oval and has a very thin skin. pl. **potatoes.**

pound¹ /pound/ *n.* Measure of weight, 16 ounces. Abbreviated **lb.**

pound² /pound/ *v.* Hit hard again and again: *pound a nail.*

practice /prak′ təs/ *n.* **1.** Action done many times over for skill. **2.** The usual way; custom. **3.** Business of a doctor or lawyer. —*v.* **1.** Do something again and again in order to learn it. **2.** Do: *Practice what you preach.* **3.** Work at or follow as a profession: *practice law or medicine.* **practiced, practicing.** Also, **practise.**

prep. *abbrev.* for *preposition.*

preposition /prep′ ə zish′ ən/ *n.* A word that shows the relationship between other words. *With* and *to* are prepositions in this sentence: *I went with them to school.*

president /prez′ ə dənt/ *n.* **1.** The chief officer of a club, company, college, etc. **2. President,** the highest officer of a modern republic like the United States.

price /prīs/ *n.* **1.** Cost to the buyer. **2.** Amount paid for any result: *The price of the victory was a thousand soldiers.* —*v.* **1.** Set the price of: *The hat is priced at $10.* **2.** Ask the price of: *Mother is pricing rugs.* **priced, pricing.**

pride /prīd/ *n.* **1.** A high opinion of one's own worth. **2.** Something one is proud of: *Her daughter is her great pride.* **3.** Pleasure in something concerning oneself.

private /prī′ vət/ *adj.* Not for the public; personal. —*n.* Soldier or marine of the lowest rank.

probable /prob′ ə bəl/ *adj.* **1.** Likely to happen:

Cooler weather is probable after rain. **2.** Likely to be true: *the probable cause of an accident.*

probably /prob′ ə blē/ *adv.* More likely than not.

program /prō′ gram/ *or* /prō′ grəm/ *n.* **1.** List of events set down in order with a list of the performers. **2.** Items making up an entertainment. **3.** Plan of what is to be done.

prompt /prompt/ *adj.* **1.** On time. **2.** Done at once: *a prompt call.* —*v.* **1.** Cause someone to do something: *His hunger prompted him to eat the candy.* **2.** Remind a speaker or actor of the words or actions needed.

pron. *abbrev.* for *pronoun.*

pronoun /prō′ noun/ *n.* Word used to point out without naming; word used instead of a noun.

prop /prop/ *n.* Thing or person used to support another. —*v.* Hold up by placing a support under or against. **propped, propping.**

protect /prō tekt′/ *v.* Shield from harm or danger.

prove /prüv/ *v.* Show that a thing is true. **proved, proving.**

provide /prō vīd′/ *v.* Supply; give what is needed or wanted. **provided, providing.**

prune¹ /prün/ *n.* A kind of sweet plum that is dried.

prune² /prün/ *v.* Cut away useless parts. **pruned, pruning.**

P.S. *abbrev.* for *postscript.*

pt. *abbrev.* for *pint. pl.* **pts.**

puddle /pud′ əl/ *n.* Small pool of liquid, especially water or dirty water.

pupil¹ /pū′ pəl/ *n.* Person who is being taught by someone.

pupil² /pū′ pəl/ *n.* The black center of the eye.

put /pùt/ *v.* Place; set: *put in place.* **put, putting.**

Qq

qt. *or* **qu.** *or* **q.** *abbrev.* for *quart. pl.* **qt.** *or* **qts.**

quart /kwärt/ *or* /kwôrt/ *n.* **1.** Measure for liquids, equal to one-fourth of a gallon. **2.** Measure for dry things equal to one-eighth of a peck.

quarter /kwôr′ tər/ *or* /kwär′ tər/ *n.* One of four equal parts; half of a half; one-fourth. —*v.* Divide into fourths.

question /kwes′ chən/ *n.* **1.** Thing asked in order to find out. **2.** Matter to be talked over. —*v.* **1.** Ask in order to find out. **2.** Doubt.

quiet /kwī′ ət/ *adj.* **1.** Making little or no noise. **2.** Not busy: *a quiet evening at home.* —*n.* Peace; stillness. —*v.* **1.** Make quiet: *The mother quieted her child.* **2.** Become quiet.

Rr

radio /rā′ dē ō/ *n.* Device for receiving and making it possible to hear sounds sent by electric waves without wires. —*v.* Send out by radio. —*adj.* Used in radio; of radio.

radish /rad′ ish/ *n.* **1.** Small, crisp root of a plant with a red or white skin, used as a relish and in salads. **2.** The plant. *pl.* **radishes.**

rail¹ /rāl/ *n.* **1.** Bar of wood or metal: *a porch rail.* **2.** Railroad: *We traveled by rail.*

rail² /rāl/ *v.* Complain bitterly: *He railed at his bad luck.*

railroad /rāl′ rōd′/ *n.* Road or track with steel rails on which the wheels of cars go.

rapid /rap′ id/ *adj.* Very quick; swift.

rather /raŦH′ ər/ *adv.* **1.** More willingly: *We would rather go along.* **2.** More truly: *I ate two, or rather three, cookies.* **3.** More than a little: *It is rather late.*

razor /rā′ zər/ *n.* Tool with sharp blade to shave with.

Rd. *abbrev.* for *road.*

re— *prefix.* **1.** Again: *reopen.* **2.** Back: *repay.*

reach /rēch/ *v.* **1.** Get to: *Your letter reached me yesterday.* **2.** Stretch out: *A hand reached out to him.* **3.** Extend: *The United States reaches from ocean to ocean.* **4.** Get in touch with: *reach by telephone.* —*n.* **1.** Power to understand: *The subject is beyond a child's reach.* **2.** The distance of reaching.

real /rē′ əl/ *adj.* **1.** Not imagined; not made up. **2.** Genuine: *real diamonds.*

reappear /rē′ ə pir′/ *v.* Come into sight again.

rearrange /rē′ ə rānj′/ *v.* Arrange in a new way. **rearranged, rearranging.**

recall /rē kôl′/ *v.* **1.** Call back to mind; remember. **2.** Take back.

recess /rē′ ses/ *or* /rə ses′/ *n.* **1.** Time during which work stops. **2.** An inner place or part: *the recesses of the cave. pl.* **recesses.** /rē ses′/ —*v.* Take a recess, or short break.

/a/ ran /ā/ rain /ã/ care /ä/ car /e/ hen /ē/ he /ėr/ her /i/ in /ī/ ice /o/ not /ō/ no /ô/ off /u/ us
/ū/ use /ü/ tool /ù/ took /ou/ cow /oi/ boy /ch/ church /hw/ when /ng/ sing /sh/ ship /ŦH/ this
/th/ thin /zh/ vision /ə/ about, taken, pencil, lemon, circus

record /rē kôrd′/ v. **1.** Set down in writing so as to keep for future use. **2.** Put sounds on a disk to be used on a phonograph. /rek′ ərd/ —n. **1.** Written account. **2.** The known facts about what has happened. **3.** The best yet done. **4.** Disk used on a phonograph.

recover /rē kuv′ ər/ v. **1.** Get back something lost, stolen, or taken away. **2.** Get well.

regular /reg′ ū lər/ adj. **1.** Usual. **2.** Following some rule or principle. **3.** Coming again and again at the same time. **4.** Well-balanced; even in size: *regular teeth.* **5.** Steady.

reindeer /rān′ dir′/ n. Kind of large deer, with branching horns, living in northern regions. pl. **reindeer.**

relate /rē lāt′/ v. Tell; give an account: *The traveler will relate her adventures.* **related, relating.**

remain /rē mān′/ v. Continue in a place; stay.

remember /rē mem′ bər/ v. **1.** Call back to mind; take care not to forget. **2.** Make a gift to: *Uncle remembered me in his will.*

remind /rē mīnd′/ v. Cause to remember.

remove /rē müv′/ v. **1.** Get rid of; put an end to. **2.** Move from a place or position. **removed, removing.**

repair /rē pãr′/ v. **1.** Mend; put in good condition again. **2.** Make up for: *repair the damage.* —n. **1.** Condition for use. **2.** Act or work of making repairs.

repeat /rē pēt′/ v. **1.** Do or make again. **2.** Say over again. **3.** Say after another says. **4.** Tell.

replace /rē plās′/ v. **1.** Put back; put in place again. **2.** Get another in place of. **3.** Take the place of. **replaced, replacing.**

reply /rē plī′/ n. Answer: *make a reply.* pl. **replies.** —v. Answer by words or actions: *reply with a shout.* **replied, replying.**

report /rē pôrt′/ n. **1.** Account of something seen, heard, or read about. **2.** Sound of an explosion or shot: *the report of a gun.* —v. **1.** Give or bring an account of; describe; tell. **2.** Present oneself: *report for work.*

rescue /res′ kū/ v. Save from danger. **rescued, rescuing.** —n. Saving or freeing from harm or danger: *the ship's rescue.*

respect /rē spekt′/ n. **1.** Honor. **2.** Care; consideration: *We should have respect for public property.* —v. **1.** Show honor or esteem for. **2.** Care for; show consideration for.

restore /rē stôr′/ v. **1.** Bring back. **2.** Bring or put back. **restored, restoring.**

retreat /rē trēt′/ v. Go back; withdraw: *The enemy retreated before the advance of our soldiers.* —n. **1.** Act of withdrawing or going back: *an orderly retreat.* **2.** A safe, quiet place.

reward /rē wôrd′/ or /rē wärd′/ n. Something given in return for something done. —v. Give a reward to.

rifle /rī′ fəl/ n. Kind of gun with long barrel, usually fired from the shoulder.

rise /rīz/ v. **1.** Get up. **2.** Go or come up: *A kite rises.* **3.** Increase: *Prices may rise.* **4.** Slope upward. **rose, risen, rising.** —n. **1.** Going up; increase. **2.** Upward slope: *the rise of the hills.*

road /rōd/ n. A way between places.

roar /rôr/ n. Loud, deep sound; noise. —v. **1.** Make a loud, deep sound. **2.** Laugh loudly: *The crowd roared at the clown's trick.*

robin /rob′ ən/ n. Large American thrush with a reddish breast.

rocket /rok′ ət/ n. Device consisting of a tube open at one end and filled with an explosive or other substance that burns rapidly so as to force the tube upward or forward.

root¹ /rüt/ n. Underground part of a plant from which other things grow. —v. Become fixed in the ground and begin to grow.

root² /rüt/ v. Cheer and support a team.

route /rüt/ or /rout/ n. Way to go; road. —v. Send by a certain way. **routed, routing.**

rude /rüd/ adj. **1.** Impolite. **2.** Coarse; rough: *a rude bed of branches.* **ruder, rudest.**

ruin /rü′ ən/ n. **1.** Building or wall that has fallen to pieces. **2.** Very great damage. **3.** A fallen or decayed condition. **4.** Downfall: *Gambling was his ruin.* —v. Destroy; spoil.

Ss

saint /sānt/ n. A very holy person.

salad /sal′ əd/ n. Raw vegetables served with a dressing. Often cold meat, fish, eggs, and cooked vegetables, or fruit are used along with or instead of raw vegetables.

salute /sə lüt′/ v. **1.** Honor in a formal manner by raising the hand to the head, by firing guns, or by dipping flags. **2.** Greet. **saluted, saluting.** —n. Act of saluting; sign of welcome or honor: *She bowed in response to the salute of the crowd.*

Sat. abbrev. for *Saturday.*

satisfy /sat′ is fī/ v. **1.** Give enough to. **2.** Make contented: *Are you satisfied now?* **3.** Convince. **satisfied, satisfying.**

Saturday /sat′ ər dā/ n. The seventh day of the week, following Friday.

sawdust /sô′ dust′/ *n.* Particles of wood made by sawing.

scarce /skãrs/ *adj.* Hard to get; rare. **scarcer, scarcest.**

scarecrow /skãr′ krō′/ *n.* Figure of man dressed in old clothes, set in a field to frighten birds away from crops.

scene /sēn/ *n.* **1.** Time, place, and circumstances of a play or story: *The scene of the story is laid in Boston.* **2.** Part of a play. **3.** Painted screens used in a theater to represent places. **4.** View; picture. **5.** Show of strong feelings in front of others: *He made a scene by screaming loudly.*

science /sī′ əns/ *n.* Knowledge based on observed facts and tested truths arranged in an orderly system.

score /skôr/ *n.* **1.** Number of points won in a game or contest. **2.** Record of points made in a game or contest. **3.** Grade on a test. **4.** Debt or wrong: *settle an old score.* **5.** Group of twenty. **6.** Written or printed piece of music. —*v.* **1.** Win points in a game. **2.** Get a certain grade on a test. **3.** Mark with lines, cuts, or notches. **scored, scoring.**

season /sē′ zən/ *n.* **1.** One of the four periods of the year: spring, summer, fall, winter. **2.** Any period or time marked by something special. —*v.* **1.** Improve the flavor of. **2.** Make or become fit for use by a period of keeping or treatment: *Wood is seasoned by drying.*

secret /sē′ krət/ *n.* Something hidden from the knowledge of others. —*adj.* Kept from the knowledge of others: *a secret weapon.*

see /sē/ *v.* **1.** Look at. **2.** Have the power of sight. **3.** Call on: *I went to see my friends.* **4.** Understand. **saw, seen, seeing.**

seed /sēd/ *n.* **1.** Part of a plant from which a flower, vegetable, or other plant grows. **2.** Beginning of anything: *the seeds of trouble.* —*v.* **1.** Scatter seeds. **2.** Remove seeds from: *Seed raisins.* **3.** Shed seeds.

seen /sēn/ *v.* See **see.** *I have seen that play.*

selfish /sel′ fish/ *adj.* Caring too much for oneself; putting one's own interests first.

separate /sep′ ə rət/ *adj.* Apart from others; not joined: *separate seats* /sep′ ə rāt′/ —*v.* **1.** Put apart; take away. **2.** Come apart: *The rope separated.* **separated, separating.**

Sept. *abbrev.* for *September.*

September /sep tem′ bər/ *n.* The ninth month of the year, following August. September has 30 days.

serious /sir′ ē əs/ *adj.* **1.** Thoughtful; grave. **2.** In earnest; not foolish. **3.** Important: *a serious matter.* **4.** Dangerous.

servant /sėr′ vənt/ *n.* **1.** Person employed in a household. **2.** Person devoted to any service: *Police officers are public servants.*

several /sev′ ər əl/ *adj.* More than two or three, but not many; a few: *several children.* —*n.* More than two or three, but not many; a few: *Several have decided to go.*

shadow /shad′ ō/ *n.* Shade made by some person, animal, or thing. —*v.* Follow closely, usually secretly: *The detective shadowed the suspected burglar.*

shape /shāp/ *n.* **1.** Form; appearance: *a round shape.* **2.** Condition: *in good shape.* —*v.* **1.** Form: *Shape the clay.* **2.** Develop: *Her plan is shaping well.* **shaped, shaping.**

she'll /shēl/ *n.* **1.** She will. **2.** She shall.

shine /shīn/ *v.* **1.** Send out light. **2.** Polish: *shine shoes.* **3.** Be bright; do very well: *He shines in sports and in school.* **shone** or **shined, shining.** —*n.* Light; brightness.

shone /shōn/ *v.* See **shine.** *The sun has not shone for a week.*

shoulder /shōl′ dər/ *n.* **1.** Part of the body to which the arm, foreleg, or wing is attached. **2.** Part of a garment that covers a shoulder. **3.** Something that sticks out like a shoulder: *Do not drive on the shoulder of the road.* —*v.* Bear burden or blame: *He shouldered the responsibility of planning the program.*

shouldn't /shùd′ ənt/ Should not.

show /shō/ *v.* **1.** Put in sight. **2.** Point out. **3.** Explain. **4.** Give; grant: *show mercy.* **5.** Display. **showed, shown** or **showed, showing.** —*n.* Any kind of public display.

shown /shōn/ *v.* See **show.** *The clerk has shown the lady many hats.*

sigh /sī/ *v.* **1.** Let out a long, deep breath because one is sad, tired, or relieved. **2.** Make a sound like a sigh. **3.** Wish very much. —*n.* Act or sound of sighing: *sigh of relief.*

sight /sīt/ *n.* **1.** Power of seeing. **2.** View; glimpse: *I caught sight of them.* **3.** Something worth seeing: *Niagara Falls is a wonderful sight.* —*v.* See: *Columbus sighted land.*

/a/ ran /ā/ rain /ä/ care /ä/ car /e/ hen /ē/ he /ėr/ her /i/ in /ī/ ice /o/ not /ō/ no /ô/ off /u/ us
/ū/ use /ü/ tool /ù/ took /ou/ cow /oi/ boy /ch/ church /hw/ when /ng/ sing /sh/ ship /ŦH/ this
/th/ thin /zh/ vision /ə/ about, taken, pencil, lemon, circus

185

sign /sīn/ *n.* **1.** Anything used to point out something: *road signs.* **2.** Indication: *signs of life.* **3.** Trace: *The hunters found signs of deer.* —*v.* Put one's name on.

signal /sig′ nəl/ *n.* Sign giving notice of something. —*v.* Make a signal to. —*adj.* Remarkable: *The airplane was a signal invention.*

silence /sī′ ləns/ *n.* Absence of sound; stillness. —*v.* Make quiet; stop the noise of. **silenced, silencing.** —*interj.* Be still!

silent /sī′ lənt/ *adj.* **1.** Quiet; still; noiseless: *a silent house.* **2.** Not said out loud: *silent reading.*

simple /sim′ pəl/ *adj.* **1.** Easy to do or understand. **2.** Plain. **3.** Weak in mind; stupid. **simpler, simplest.**

sing. *abbrev.* for *singular.*

singular /sing′ gū lər/ *adj.* One in number: Girl *is singular. Girls is plural.* —*n.* The singular number in grammar: Ox *is the singular of* oxen.

skid /skid/ *v.* Slip or slide sideways while moving. **skidded, skidding.** —*n.* A sideways slip or slide.

skill /skil/ *n.* Ability to do things well with one's body or with tools: *It takes skill to tune a piano.*

skyline /skī′ līn′/ *n.* **1.** Line at which earth and sky seem to meet; horizon. **2.** Outline of buildings against the sky.

sled /sled/ *n.* Framework of boards mounted on runners for use on snow and ice. —*v.* Ride on a sled. **sledded, sledding.**

sleep /slēp/ *v.* Rest body and mind; be without ordinary thought or movement: *We sleep at night.* **slept, sleeping.** —*n.* Rest of body and mind: *a deep sleep.*

slept /slept/ *v. See* **sleep.** *The child slept soundly through the night.*

slice /slīs/ *n.* Thin, flat piece cut from something. —*v.* Cut into slices. **sliced, slicing.**

slight /slīt/ *adj.* **1.** Not important: *a slight headache.* **2.** Slender. —*n.* An act showing lack of respect. —*v.* Neglect: *Do not slight the guests.*

slim /slim/ *adj.* **1.** Thin. **2.** Small; slight: *a slim chance.* **slimmer, slimmest.** —*v.* Make or become slim. **slimmed, slimming.**

smooth /smū̵H/ *adj.* **1.** Flat; level. **2.** Without lumps or roughness. **3.** Pleasant. —*v.* Make flat, even, or level: *smooth a dress.*

snake /snāk/ *n.* Long, slender, crawling reptile.

snurk /snėrk/ *n.* A word that has an unexpected spelling, for example, *have* or *gone.*

soar /sôr/ *v.* **1.** Fly upward. **2.** Rise beyond what is common: *Prices are soaring.*

soil¹ /soil/ *n.* Ground; earth; dirt.

soil² /soil/ *v.* **1.** Make dirty: *She soiled her dress.* **2.** Become dirty: *White gloves soil easily.*

soldier /sōl′ jər/ *n.* **1.** Person who serves in an army. **2.** Person who serves in a cause.

sore /sôr/ *adj.* **1.** Painful. **2.** Sad: *The suffering of the poor makes her heart sore.* **3.** Angry: *He is sore about missing the game.* —*n.* Place on the body where the skin is bruised or broken.

south /south/ *n.* **1.** Direction just opposite north. **2.** Part of any country toward the south. —*adj.* From the south: *a south wind.* —*adv.* Toward the south: *Drive south forty miles.*

soybean /soi′ bēn′/ *n.* **1.** Bean grown in Asia and North America. **2.** The plant it grows on.

spare /spâr/ *v.* **1.** Show mercy to: *spare the enemy.* **2.** Get along without: *spare the car for tonight.* **spared, sparing.** —*adj.* **1.** Extra: *spare tire; spare time.* **2.** Thin; lean: *Lincoln was a spare man.* **sparer, sparest.**

speech /spēch/ *n.* **1.** Talk. **2.** Power of speaking: *Animals lack speech.* **3.** A public talk. **4.** Language. *pl.* **speeches.**

spell¹ /spel/ *v.* Write or say the letters of a word in order. **spelled** *or* **spelt, spelling.**

spell² /spel/ *n.* **1.** Words supposed to have magic power. **2.** Charm: *the spell of beautiful music.*

spell³ /spel/ *n.* Period of time: *The child had a spell of coughing.*

spinach /spin′ əch/ *n.* A plant whose green leaves are boiled and eaten.

spoon /spün/ *n.* Small, shallow bowl at the end of a handle, used to take up or stir food.

spray¹ /sprā/ *n.* **1.** Liquid going through the air in small drops. **2.** Instrument that sends out liquid as a spray. —*v.* Sprinkle.

spray² /sprā/ *n.* Small branch of a plant with its leaves, flowers, or fruit.

sprinkle /spring′ kəl/ *v.* **1.** Scatter in tiny bits. **2.** Spray in small drops. **3.** Rain a little. **sprinkled, sprinkling.** —*n.* A light rain.

squeeze /skwēz/ *v.* **1.** Press hard. **2.** Hug. **squeezed, squeezing.** —*n.* **1.** Tight pressure: *She gave my arm a squeeze.* **2.** Crowd: *Five people in one car will be a tight squeeze.*

St. *abbrev.* for **1.** Street. **2.** Saint.

stall¹ /stôl/ *n.* **1.** Place in a stable for one animal. **2.** A small place for selling things: *stalls in the market.* —*v.* Stop, usually against one's will: *The engine stalled.*

stall² /stôl/ *v.* Delay: *You have been stalling long enough.*

statement /stāt′ mənt/ *n.* **1.** Something stated or said; report. **2.** A sentence that is not a command or question.

station /stā′ shən/ **1.** Regular stopping place. **2.** Place for sending out or receiving programs or messages by radio or television. —*v.* Place: *He stationed himself near the door.*

steal /stēl/ *v.* **1.** Take something dishonestly. **2.** Move secretly or quietly: *She stole out of the house.* **stole, stolen, stealing.**

steel /stēl/ *n.* Iron mixed with carbon so that it is very hard, strong, and tough. —*adj.* Made of steel. —*v.* Make hard or strong like steel: *He steeled himself to withstand the pain.*

stew /stū/ *or* /stü/ *v.* Cook by slow boiling. —*n.* Food cooked by slow boiling: *beef stew.*

sting /sting/ *v.* **1.** Prick with a small point: *Bees sting.* **2.** Cause a feeling like a sting. **3.** Cause sadness. **stung, stinging.** —*n.* **1.** Sharp pain. **2.** Prick; wound.

stole /stōl/ *v. See* **steal.** *Who stole my money?*

stomach /stum′ ək/ *n.* **1.** Large, muscular bag in the body which first receives the food and digests some of it before passing it on to the intestines. **2.** Part of the body containing the stomach.

store /stôr/ *n.* **1.** Place where goods are kept for sale: *a clothing store.* **2.** Something put away for later use: *a store of vegetables.* **3.** Place where things are kept for future use. —*v.* **1.** Supply or stock. **2.** Put away for use later. **3.** Put in a warehouse or place used for preserving. **stored, storing.**

street /strēt/ *n.* Road in a city or town, usually with buildings on both sides.

strike /strīk/ *v.* **1.** Hit. **2.** Set on fire by hitting or rubbing: *Strike a match.* **3.** Find suddenly: *strike oil.* **4.** Stop work to get better pay or force an employer to meet a demand. **struck, striking.** —*n.* **1.** Sudden success in finding ore or oil. **2.** Stopping of work to force an employer to meet a demand: *The workers were home during the strike.*

stripe /strīp/ *n.* A long, narrow band. —*v.* Mark with stripes. **striped, striping.**

stroke¹ /strōk/ *n.* **1.** Blow: *a stroke of the hammer.* **2.** Mark made by a pen, pencil, or brush. **3.** A single movement made again and again: *She swims with a fast stroke.* **4.** A very successful effort: *a stroke of good fortune.*

stroke² /strōk/ *v.* Move the hand gently along: *She stroked the kitten.* **stroked, stroking.**

student /stūd′ ənt/ *or* /stüd′ ənt/ *n.* **1.** Person who studies: *She is a student of birds.* **2.** Person who is studying in a school or college.

stumble /stum′ bəl/ *v.* **1.** Slip or trip. **2.** Walk in an unsteady way. **3.** Speak or act in a clumsy way: *He stumbled through his speech.* **stumbled, stumbling.**

subject /sub′ jəkt/ *n.* **1.** Something thought about, discussed, or studied. **2.** Person under the control of another. **3.** Word or words about which something is said in a sentence. /sub jekt′/ —*v.* **1.** Bring under control, power: *Rome subjected all Italy to her rule.* **2.** Cause to undergo or experience something.

success /sək ses′/ *n.* **1.** A favorable result; good fortune. **2.** Person or thing that succeeds. *pl.* **successes.**

suit /sūt/ *or* /süt/ *n.* **1.** Set of clothes. **2.** A case in a court of law. —*v.* **1.** Make fit: *suit the punishment to the crime.* **2.** Fit: *Which time suits you?*

suitcase /sūt′ kās′/ *n.* Flat traveling bag: *Her suitcase was too small to hold her coat.*

Sun. *abbrev.* for *Sunday.*

sunburn /sun′ bėrn′/ *n.* Burning the skin by the sun's rays. —*v.* Become burned by the sun. **sunburned** or **sunburnt, sunburning.**

Sunday /sun′ dā/ *n.* The first day of the week.

sunshine /sun′ shīn/ *n.* **1.** The light of the sun. **2.** Cheerfulness; happiness.

superintendent /sü′ pər in ten′ dənt/ *n.* **1.** Person who directs; manager. **2.** Supervisor.

supply /sə plī′/ *v.* Furnish; provide. **supplied, supplying.** —*n.* Quantity ready for use; stock on hand. *pl.* **supplies.**

Supt. *abbrev.* for *superintendent.*

suspect /sus pekt′/ *v.* Imagine to be so; believe guilty. /sus′ pekt/ —*n.* Person suspected.

sweet /swēt/ *adj.* **1.** Having a taste like sugar or honey. **2.** Pleasant: *a sweet smile.* **3.** Fresh; not spoiled: *sweet milk.* —*n.* Something sweet; candy.

sword /sôrd/ *n.* Weapon, usually metal, with a long, sharp blade fixed in a handle or hilt.

syllable /sil′ ə bəl/ *n.* Word or part of a word pronounced as a unit that usually consists of a vowel alone or a vowel with one or more consonants.

/a/ ran /ā/ rain /ã/ care /ä/ car /e/ hen /ē/ he /ėr/ her /i/ in /ī/ ice /o/ not /ō/ no /ô/ off /u/ us
/ū/ use /ü/ tool /u̇/ took /ou/ cow /oi/ boy /ch/ church /hw/ when /ng/ sing /sh/ ship /ᴛʜ/ this
/th/ thin /zh/ vision /ə/ about, taken, pencil, lemon, circus

syn. *abbrev.* for *synonym.*

synonym /sin′ ə nim/ *n.* Word that means the same or nearly the same as another word: Large *and* big *are synonyms.*

Tt

teach /tēch/ *v.* **1.** Help to learn. **2.** Give lessons. **taught, teaching.**

teapot /tē′ pot′/ *n.* Container with a handle and a spout for making and serving tea.

teaspoon /tē′ spün′/ *n.* Spoon smaller than a tablespoon, commonly used to stir tea or coffee.

teeth /tēth/ *n. pl.* More than one tooth.

telephone /tel′ ə fōn/ *n.* Apparatus, system, or process for sending sound or speech over wires by means of electricity. —*v.* Talk through a telephone. **telephoned, telephoning.**

television /tel′ ə vizh′ ən/ *n.* **1.** Process of sending pictures through the air by electricity. **2.** Apparatus on which these pictures may be seen.

terrible /ter′ ə bəl/ *adj.* Causing great fear; dreadful; awful.

that's /ᴛʜats/ That is.

thaw /thô/ *v.* **1.** Melt. **2.** Become less cold, less formal: *His shyness thawed under kindness.* —*n.* Weather above the freezing point.

there's /ᴛʜãrz/ There is.

they'll /ᴛʜāl/ **1.** They will. **2.** They shall.

they've /ᴛʜāv/ They have.

thief /thēf/ *n.* Person who steals, especially one who steals secretly. *pl.* **thieves.**

thigh /thī/ *n.* Part of the leg between the hip and knee.

think /thingk/ *v.* **1.** Have ideas; use the mind: *You must learn to think clearly.* **2.** Have in the mind. **3.** Have an opinion; believe. **4.** Reflect: *I want to think before answering that question.* **5.** Consider. **6.** Imagine. **7.** Expect: *I did not think to find you here.* **thought, thinking.**

thirsty /thėr′ stē/ *adj.* **1.** Feeling thirst; having thirst. **2.** Without water or moisture; dry: *The plant seems thirsty.* **thirstier, thirstiest.**

thought /thôt/ *v.* See **think.** *We thought it would rain.*

thousand /thou′ zənd/ *n.* and *adj.* Ten hundred; 1000: *A thousand is ten times a hundred.*

thread /thred/ *n.* Cotton, silk, flax, or some similar material spun out into a fine cord. —*v.* Pass a thread through: *thread a needle.*

through /thrü/ *prep.* **1.** Between the parts of.

2. Here and there in; over. **3.** By means of. **4.** Finished with. —*adj.* Going all the way without change: *a through train.* —*adv.* **1.** Finished. **2.** From beginning to end.

throughout /thrü out′/ *prep.* In every part; through all.

Thurs. *abbrev.* for *Thursday.*

Thursday /thėrz′ dā/ *n.* The fifth day of the week, following Wednesday.

ticket /tik′ ət/ *n.* **1.** Card that gives its holder a right or privilege. **2.** Summons to appear in court, given to one who has broken a traffic law. **3.** Card or piece of paper attached to something to show its price, what it is, or some similar information. —*v.* Put a ticket on.

tide /tīd/ *n.* The rise and fall of the ocean about every twelve hours, caused by the attraction of the moon and sun.

tie /tī/ *v.* Fasten with a string or the like; bind. **tied, tying.** —*n.* Necktie.

tied /tīd/ *v.* See **tie.** *She tied the rope tightly.*

tiger /tī′ gər/ *n.* Large, fierce animal with dull yellow fur striped with black.

tight /tīt/ *adj.* **1.** Firm: *a tight knot.* **2.** Fitting closely. **3.** Close: *a tight race.* **4.** Stingy. —*adv.* Firmly: *The rope was tied too tight.*

—tion *suffix* used to form *nouns.* **1.** Act or process of ____ing: *Attention* means *act or process of attending.* **2.** Condition of being ____ed: *Exhaustion* means *condition of being exhausted.*

toast /tōst/ *n.* Slices of bread browned by heat. —*v.* **1.** Brown by heat. **2.** Heat: *They toasted their feet before the fire.*

toe /tō/ *n.* **1.** One of the five end parts of the foot. **2.** The part of a stocking, shoe, or slipper that covers the toes. —*v.* Touch with the toes: *toe a line.* **toed, toeing.**

together /tə geᴛʜ′ ər/ *adv.* **1.** With each other: *walk together.* **2.** Into one gathering.

tomato /tə mā′ tō/ *n.* Juicy fruit used as a vegetable. Most tomatoes are red, but some are yellow. *pl.* **tomatoes.**

tongue /tung/ *n.* Movable piece of flesh in the mouth.

tool /tül/ *n.* An instrument used in doing work.

topsoil /top′ soil′/ *n.* The upper part of the soil; surface soil.

total /tō′ təl/ *adj.* **1.** Whole; entire: *total cost; total amount.* **2.** Complete: *total darkness.* —*n.* Whole amount. —*v.* Find the sum of; add: *total the column of figures.*

tow /tō/ *v.* Pull by a rope or chain. —*n.* **1.** What is towed: *Each tug has a tow of three barges.*

2. Act of towing. **3.** Rope or chain used in towing.

toward /tôrd/, /tōrd/, *or* /tə wôrd′/ *prep.* **1.** In the direction of. **2.** With respect to: *an attitude toward war.* **3.** Near. **4.** For: *a donation toward the school library.*

tractor /trak′ tər/ *n.* Engine that moves on wheels, used for pulling wagons, plows, or other vehicles.

traffic /traf′ ik/ *n.* People, cars, wagons, ships, or the like coming and going along a way of travel. —*v.* Carry on trade; buy; sell; exchange: *The sailors trafficked with the natives for ivory.* **trafficked, trafficking.**

trap /trap/ *n.* **1.** Thing or means for catching animals. **2.** Trick or other ways for catching someone off guard. —*v.* Catch in a trap: *The rabbit was trapped.* **trapped, trapping.**

tray /trā/ *n.* A flat holder or container with a rim around it: *The waiter carried a tray.*

treasure /trezh′ ər/ *n.* **1.** Wealth or riches stored up; valuable things. **2.** Any thing or person that is much valued. —*v.* Value highly: *She treasured the old watch.* **treasured, treasuring.**

trial /trī′ əl/ *n.* **1.** Examining and deciding a case in court. **2.** Process of trying and testing: *He gave the machine another trial.* **3.** Hardship; trouble: *She had many trials in her life.* —*adj.* For a test: *a trial trip.*

tried /trīd/ *v.* See **try.** *We tried our best to be on time.*

trouble /trub′ əl/ *n.* **1.** Worry; difficulty. **2.** Extra work; bother. **3.** Illness: *stomach trouble.* —*v.* **1.** Disturb. **2.** Cause extra work or effort to: *Don't trouble yourself to do this extra work.* **troubled, troubling.**

true /trü/ *adj.* **1.** Not false: *a true story.* **2.** Real: *true gold.* **3.** Faithful: *a true friend.* —*adv.* Exactly: *Her words ring true.*

truth /trüth/ *n.* That which is true.

try /trī/ *v.* **1.** Make an effort. **2.** Test: *Try this car before you buy it.* **3.** Investigate in a court of law: *He was tried and found guilty of robbery.* **4.** Strain: *Don't try your eyes by reading in poor light.* **tried, trying.** —*n.* Attempt: *He made three tries at the high jump.*

Tues. *abbrev.* for *Tuesday.*

Tuesday /tüz′ dā/ *or* /tüz′ dā/ *n.* The third day of the week, following Monday.

tune /tün/ *or* /tün/ *n.* **1.** Melody. **2.** Proper pitch: *The piano is out of tune.* —*v.* Put in tune: *tune a piano.* **tuned, tuning.**

TV *abbrev.* for *television.*

Uu

un— *prefix* **1.** Not ____: *Unchanged* means *not changed.* **2.** Do the opposite of ____: *Unfasten* means *the opposite of fasten.*

unfold /un fōld′/ *v.* **1.** Open the folds of; spread out. **2.** Explain; show. **3.** Open.

unhappy /un hap′ ē/ *adj.* Without gladness; sad; sorrowful. **unhappier, unhappiest.**

unlike /un līk′/ *adj.* Not like, different.

unload /un lōd′/ *v.* Remove a load from.

unlock /un lok′/ *v.* Open the lock of; open anything firmly closed.

unlucky /un luk′ ē/ *adj.* Not lucky; unfortunate; bringing bad luck. **unluckier, unluckiest.**

untie /un tī′/ *v.* Unfasten; undo. **untied, untying.**

upstairs /up′ stãrz′/ *adv.* On an upper floor. —*n.* An upper floor.

urge /ėrj/ *v.* **1.** Push; force; drive. **2.** Plead with. **urged, urging.** —*n.* A driving force: *The urge of hunger made him beg for food.*

useless /ūs′ ləs/ *adj.* Of no use; worthless.

usual /ū′ zhü əl/ *adj.* In common use; customary.

Vv

v. *abbrev.* for *verb.*

vacant /vā′ kənt/ *adj.* Empty; not filled; not occupied: *a vacant space; a vacant chair.*

vanish /van′ ish/ *v.* Disappear; disappear suddenly.

vegetable /vej′ ə tə bəl/ *n.* Plant whose fruit, seeds, roots, or other parts are used for food.

verb /vėrb/ *n.* Word that tells what is or what is done; part of speech that expresses action or being.

versus /vėr′ səs/ *prep.* Against: *The lawsuit is Clay versus Jones.*

view /vū/ *n.* **1.** Sight: *our first view of the ocean.* **2.** Scene. **3.** Option. —*v.* **1.** See. **2.** Consider.

violin /vī ə lin′/ *n.* Musical instrument with four strings played with a bow.

vs. *abbrev.* for *versus.*

/a/ ran /ā/ rain /ã/ care /ä/ car /e/ hen /ē/ he /ėr/ her /i/ in /ī/ ice /o/ not /ō/ no /ô/ off /u/ us
/ū/ use /ü/ tool /ù/ took /ou/ cow /oi/ boy /ch/ church /hw/ when /ng/ sing /sh/ ship /FH/ this
/th/ thin /zh/ vision /ə/ about, taken, pencil, lemon, circus

Ww

waist /wāst/ *n.* **1.** Part of the body between the ribs and hips. **2.** Part of a garment covering the body from the shoulders to the hips.

wait /wāt/ *v.* **1.** Stay or stop until something happens. **2.** Delay; put off. —*n.* Time of waiting: *a long wait.*

warehouse /wãr′ hous′/ *n.* Storehouse.

wasn't /woz′ ənt/ *or* /wuz′ ənt/ Was not.

waste /wāst/ *n.* Useless or worthless material. —*adj.* Bare; wild: *waste land.* —*v.* Make poor use of. **wasted, wasting.**

weather /weᴛʜ′ ər/ *n.* Condition of the air around or above a certain place. —*v.* Expose to the weather: *weathered wood.*

wed /wed/ *v.* **1.** Marry. **2.** Unite. **wedded, wedding** *or* **wed, wedding.**

Wed. *abbrev.* for *Wednesday.*

wedding /wed′ ing/ *n.* Marriage ceremony. —*adj.* Of a wedding: *wedding ring.*

Wednesday /wenz′ dā/ *n.* The fourth day of the week, following Tuesday.

weight /wāt/ *n.* **1.** How heavy a thing is. **2.** Piece of metal used in weighing things. **3.** Load or burden. **4.** Heaviness: *Gas has very little weight.* —*v.* Load or add weight to.

welcome /wel′ kəm/ *v.* Greet kindly. **welcomed, welcoming.** —*n.* **1.** Kind reception: *You will always have a welcome here.* **2.** Greeting. —*adj.* Gladly received: *welcome visitors.* —*interj.* Exclamation of greeting.

well-made /wel′ mād′/ *adj.* Skillfully made; sturdily built: *a well-made desk.*

we're /wir/ We are.

weren't /wėrnt/ Were not.

what's /hwots/ **1.** What is. **2.** What has.

wheat /hwēt/ *n.* **1.** The grain from which flour is made. **2.** The plant that the grain grows on.

where's /hwãrz/ **1.** Where is. **2.** Where has.

whether /hweᴛʜ′ ər/ *conj.* **1.** If: *He asked whether he might be excused.* **2.** Either: *Whether sick or well, she is cheerful.*

whine /hwīn/ *n.* A low, complaining cry. —*v.* **1.** Make a low, complaining cry. **2.** Complain in a childish way. **whined, whining.**

whirl /hwėrl/ *v.* **1.** Turn or swing round and round; spin. **2.** Move round and round: *whirl a lasso.* **3.** Move or carry quickly: *We were whirled away in an airplane.* **4.** Feel dizzy or confused. —*n.* **1.** A whirling movement. **2.** Dizzy or confused condition: *My thoughts are in a whirl.* **3.** A rapid round of happenings.

whistle /hwis′ əl/ *v.* Make a clear, shrill sound. **whistled, whistling.** —*n.* An instrument for making whistling sounds.

whom /hüm/ *pron.* What person; which person: *Whom do you like best?*

who's /hüz/ **1.** Who is. **2.** Who has.

widow /wid′ ō/ *n.* A woman whose husband has died. —*v.* Make a widow.

windshield /wind′ shēld′/ *n.* Sheet of glass to keep off the wind.

windy /win′ dē/ *adj.* Having much wind: *a windy street.* **windier, windiest.**

wise /wīz/ *adj.* Having or showing knowledge and good judgment: *a wise person.*

wolf /wu̇lf/ *n.* Wild animal somewhat like a dog. *pl.* **wolves.** —*v.* Eat greedily.

woman /wu̇m′ ən/ *n.* Female human being. A woman is a girl grown up. *pl.* **women.**

women /wim′ ən/ *n.* Plural of **woman.**

wonderful /wun′ dər fəl/ *adj.* **1.** Marvelous; remarkable. **2.** Splendid; fine.

world /wėrld/ *n.* **1.** The earth. **2.** All people.

worm /wėrm/ *n.* Small, crawling animal. —*v.* **1.** Move like a worm. **2.** Get by secret means: *They wormed their way into our confidence.*

worry /wėr′ ē/ *v.* **1.** Be uneasy. **2.** Bother; annoy. **worried, worrying.** —*n.* Care; trouble: *Worry kept her awake. pl.* **worries.**

worse /wėrs/ *adj.* Less well; more ill; more evil.

worth /wėrth/ *n.* **1.** Importance: *the worth of the painting.* **2.** Value: *your money's worth.* **3.** Quantity a certain amount of money will buy: *a dollar's worth.* —*adj.* **1.** Good enough for: *worth buying.* **2.** Equal in value to.

wouldn't /wu̇d′ ənt/ Would not.

wreck /rek/ *n.* **1.** Destruction or serious injury. **2.** What is left of anything that has been much injured. —*v.* Cause the ruin of.

wren /ren/ *n.* A small songbird.

wrestle /res′ əl/ *v.* Try to throw an opponent to the ground; struggle with. **wrestled, wrestling.**

Yy

yard /yärd/ *n.* Measure of length; 36 inches; 3 feet.

yd. *abbrev.* for *yard. pl.* **yd.** or **yds.**

yourself /yu̇r self′/ *pron.* **1.** Form of *you* used to make a statement stronger: *You yourself know the story is true.* **2.** Form used instead of *you: Did you hurt yourself?* **3.** Your real or true self. *pl.* **yourselves.**

you've /ūv/ You have.